SYMBOL AND IMAGE IN WILLIAM BLAKE

Oxford University Press, Ely House, London W. 1

GLASGOW NEW YORK TORONTO MELBOURNE WELLINGTON
CAPE TOWN SALISBURY IBADAN NAIROBI LUSAKA ADDIS ABABA
BOMBAY CALCUTTA MADRAS KARACHI LAHORE DACCA
KUALA LUMPUR HONG KONG TOKYO

SYMBOL AND IMAGE IN WILLIAM BLAKE

BY

GEORGE WINGFIELD DIGBY

KEEPER IN THE VICTORIA AND ALBERT MUSEUM

OXFORD
AT THE CLARENDON PRESS

FIRST PUBLISHED 1957
REPRINTED LITHOGRAPHICALLY IN GREAT BRITAIN
AT THE UNIVERSITY PRESS, OXFORD
FROM CORRECTED SHEETS OF THE FIRST EDITION
BY VIVIAN RIDLER
PRINTER TO THE UNIVERSITY
1967

TO

CORNELIA

IN LOVE

AND GRATITUDE

ACKNOWLEDGEMENTS

MY thanks are due to Sir Geoffrey Keynes for information he has kindly given me on several occasions; to Mr. Philip Hofer of the Fogg Museum and Harvard Library for helping me to procure photographs from American collections; and to Dr. Johann Hell for his opinion on the technical details of the Arlington Court picture, which he restored.

I am particularly grateful to Mr. Charles H. Gibbs-Smith for his help in proof-reading and in compiling the index. In the translation of the German text of H. Zimmer's book I was greatly assisted by my wife.

For the illustrations reproduced here I am indebted to the Trustees of the British Museum and the Tate Gallery, and to the Directors of the Victoria and Albert Museum, the Fitzwilliam Museum, Cambridge, the Museum of Fine Arts, Boston, the Fogg Museum, Cambridge, Mass., to the National Trust, and to Messrs. Faber and Faber Ltd. For the long quotation from Heinrich Zimmer's *Kuntsform und Yoga im indischen Kultbild* I make acknowledgements to the Frankfurter Verlags-Anstalt A-G in Berlin, and for quotations from C. G. Jung to Routledge and Kegan Paul.

CONTENTS

LIST OF ILLUSTRATIONS

(at end)

NOTE: *The Gates of Paradise* engravings are reproduced from the first edition of 1793 (British Museum copy) except for Figures 1 and 19 which are from the second edition of *c.* 1818 (British Museum, Carthew copy).

INTRODUCTION

THIS book is based on three lectures which were given at the Victoria and Albert Museum in February 1954; they have been considerably expanded, especially the third lecture which here forms Chapter II. The third chapter has been added.

The book is a study of the meaning of Blake's art based on *The Gates of Paradise* and the newly found picture at Arlington Court, with reference to nearly sixty other designs and paintings by him, all of which are reproduced here.

Chapter I is an elucidation of Blake's symbols and ideas presented in the form of a commentary on *The Gates of Paradise*, his picture sequence which bears this title. It is a picture-book of sixteen engraved plates, with an additional frontispiece and epilogue (with an eighteenth picture inset). The original edition of *The Gates of Paradise* contained only the sixteen pictures and frontispiece; it was engraved in 1793, when Blake was aged thirty-five. The second edition was engraved in about the year 1818, when Blake was aged sixty, and to this edition he added a short text of rhyming couplets and some additional inscriptions below the pictures. This text consists of a prologue of six couplets; twenty-four couplets which refer specifically to the sequence of sixteen pictures; and an epilogue of eight lines with picture inset. The whole of this is reproduced here in the illustrations, except for the twenty-four couplets of text, which form two engraved plates in Blake's second edition. The complete text will, however, be found printed on pages 1–3, preceding Chapter I; this has been transcribed from the British Museum (A. G. E. Carthew) copy. It should be noted that the illustrations given here are taken from the 1793 edition (with the exception of the first and last, figs. 1 and 19), whilst the inscriptions below the pictures are quoted as they appear in the second edition.

The Gates of Paradise is a pictorial treatise on the life of man and how he may regain that state called variously: paradise, salvation, integration, regeneration, or enlightenment. It is very representative of Blake's thought, but its concise and epigrammatic style makes it difficult to understand; at least it is difficult to appreciate its full meaning without reference to the wide background of Blake's creative work expressed in his Prophetic Books, poems, and pictorial art. Even more important than this is the right understanding of Blake's symbols and images; they are the language by means of which the intuitive imagination expresses itself, and for Blake this was a live language, not a dead one. What this means is explained in the commentary and elucidation offered here, which relates *The Gates of Paradise* with the wider scope of Blake's work, pictorial and poetic.

Chapter II is a detailed interpretation of the very important picture which came to light at Arlington Court in Devon in 1948, and which now belongs to the National Trust. It is a water-colour, with extensive use of body colour, painted on thick paper on a prepared ground of thin gesso; it therefore has the highly finished quality of a miniature painting. It measures 16 × 19½ inches, is signed and dated 'W. Blake inventor 1821', and is in its original plain gilt frame with slightly curved glass. The frame was packed with a sheet of *The Times* of 11 January 1820, and on the back was written the address of James Linnell, frame-maker and gilder, who was the father of the artist-friend and patron of Blake's last years.

Although the existence of this picture was never suspected—it came to light by chance at Arlington Court, when it was discovered in a pile of rubbish in a store-room—it is undoubtedly of paramount importance. It was painted in Blake's last phase of full maturity, about the time he was working on the Job engravings, the year after the illustrations to Thornton's Virgil and the Laocoon engraving, and four years before he began the illustrations to Dante. This picture is, in my view, one of Blake's greatest works of art and represents the central theme of all his art, namely regeneration. It is, therefore, complementary to *The Gates of Paradise* sequence, where this theme is unfolded in quite a different way, and the three phases:

the Gates of Paradise, the Door of Death, and Regeneration (which were the titles of my three lectures) are evident in each.

The Arlington Court Picture of Regeneration has been described by Geoffrey Keynes in *Studies in Art and Literature for Belle da Costa Greene* (edited by Dorothy Miner, Princeton University Press, 1954) under the title of 'Blake's Vision of the Circle of the Life of Man'. Keynes has pointed out that there is a rough pencil drawing for this picture in the Pierpont Morgan Library, which he there reproduces. The picture which was in a good state of preservation has been cleaned by Dr. Johan Hell who has kindly described its technical process for me, as given here.

A few explanatory remarks are necessary for those not familiar with Blake's work and his method of execution. His poems and his Prophetic Books (as the long mythical poems are usually called) were never printed and published in the ordinary way during his lifetime. They were etched by him on copper plates, by a special process of relief etching, and then printed on his hand-press, and thereafter usually elaborately coloured by hand. The pages of his Prophetic Books are therefore numbered as plates, according to the etched plates from which they were printed. It is important to realize that a plate of one of his Prophetic Books may be a page of text, a page of illustration, or, as is frequently the case, part text, part illustration. Also, it must be remembered that Blake did not always assemble these plates in the same order in his Prophetic Books (and in the *Songs of Innocence and Experience*), nor does each copy contain the full number of plates or pages. For instance, of the four extant copies of *Milton* two have forty-five plates or pages, one has forty-nine, and one fifty; but fifty-one plates are known to exist, as the Preface (one plate) is omitted in the two larger editions. For this reason all my references to plates of the text of the Prophetic Books refer to the standard printed edition, edited by Geoffrey Keynes and published by the Nonesuch Press in three volumes (1925). But in the case of an illustrated or pictorial plate, wherever I have cited and reproduced this as a picture, I have given the reference to the particular copy of the Prophetic Book in question. I have used the Fitzwilliam Museum and British Museum copies of *The Marriage of Heaven & Hell*, *Visions of the Daughters of Albion*, *America*, *Europe*, and *Milton*. (Details will be found given in the List of Illustrations and the Notes and References to each chapter.) Since the only coloured version of *Jerusalem* extant (the Stirling copy) is in America, I have used the splendid coloured facsimile recently published by the Blake Trust for my reproductions. The Trust's black and white facsimile of *Jerusalem*, which includes a printed text as well, can be specially recommended for the reading and study of this work, where pictorial design and poetry are so closely wedded (the Trianon Press, 1952). *The Gates of Paradise* is made up of engravings done in the normal way, including the text, and reproduced privately by Blake. The copy in the British Museum has been used. *The Illustrations of the Book of Job* were also done as engravings, but were more widely published as a subscribed edition; the engraved copper plates are in the British Museum.

The List of Illustrations shows the particular version of each picture which has been reproduced. Blake's colour prints, like his illuminated books, were done by a special technique of his own, which entailed reproduction from a basic original, but with a great deal of individual work devoted to each copy. Several extant copies of most of the colour prints are known. Many of the water-colours were also repeated, with more or less variation, for Blake's own pleasure, or for special orders. Blake also reproduced favourite designs from the Prophetic Books, which are thus sometimes found as separate pictures; for example, the two illustrations from the *Visions of the Daughters of Albion* are reproduced here from individual pictures, done in opaque colours, and now at the Tate Gallery.

The footnotes and notes at the end of the text supply the context of all passages and phrases quoted from Blake's writings. They also contain further citations and comments, where these seemed necessary. By this means I have endeavoured as far as possible to keep the text clear and readable, and not to break the thread of the narrative and the development of the ideas.

Blake's special names and phrases for personages and ideas are spelt throughout with an initial capital. Titles of his works, and all quotations from them, are given in italics. In Chapter I, however, I have reserved italics exclusively for the text of *The Gates of Paradise,* and the underlines to its pictures, whenever cited, whether in whole or in part. This seemed necessary in a detailed commentary, where it is essential for the reader to be able to distinguish at a glance between the basic text and extraneous quotations.

Such Visions have appeared to me as I my ordered race have run. (Jerusalem, plate 26)

Again he speaks in thunder and in fire!
Thunder of Thought, and flames of fierce desire.
(Jerusalem, plate 3)

Attempting to be more than Man we become less.
(The Four Zoas, Book 9, line 709)

To cleanse the Face of my Spirit by Self-examination
To bathe in the Waters of Life, to wash off the Not Human.
(Milton, plate 47, line 37–plate 48, line 1)

THE GATES OF PARADISE

For the Sexes

Mutual Forgiveness of each Vice
Such are the Gates of Paradise
Against the Accuser's chief desire
Who walked among the Stones of Fire
Jehovah's Finger Wrote the Law
Then Wept: then rose in Zeal & Awe
And in the midst of Sinai's heat
Hid it beneath his Mercy Seat
O Christians Christians! tell me Why
You rear it on your Altars high.

The Keys

The Catterpiller on the Leaf
Reminds thee of thy Mothers Grief

of the Gates

1 *My Eternal Man set in Repose*
The Female from his darkness rose
And She found me beneath a Tree
A Mandrake & in her Veil hid me
Serpent Reasonings us entice
Of Good & Evil: Virtue & Vice
2 *Doubt Self Jealous Watry folly*
3 *Struggling thro Earths Melancholy*
4 *Naked in Air in Shame & Fear*
5 *Blind in Fire with shield & spear*

Two Horn'd Reasoning Cloven Fiction
In Doubt which is Self contradiction
A dark Hermaphrodite I stood
Rational Truth Root of Evil & Good
Round me flew the Flaming Sword
Round her snowy Whirlwinds roard
Freezing her Veil the Mundane Shell
6 *I rent the Veil where the Dead dwell*
When weary Man enters his Cave
He meets his Saviour in the Grave
Some find a Female Garment there
And some a Male woven with care
Lest the Sexual Garments sweet
Should grow a devouring Winding sheet
7 *One Dies! Alas! the Living & Dead*
One is slain & One is fled
8 *In Vain-glory hatcht & nurst*
By double Spectres Self Accurst
My Son! My Son! thou treatest me
But as I have instructed thee
9 *On the shadows of the Moon*
Climbing thro Nights highest noon
10 *In Times Ocean falling drownd*
In Aged Ignorance profound
11 *Holy & cold I clipd the Wings*
Of all Sublunary Things
12 *And in depths of my Dungeons*
Closed the Father & the Sons
13 *But when once I did descry*
The Immortal Man that cannot Die
14 *Thro evening shades I haste away*
To close the Labours of my Day
15 *The Door of Death I open found*
And the Worm Weaving in the Ground
16 *Thou'rt my Mother from the Womb*

Wife Sister Daughter to the Tomb
Weaving to Dreams the Sexual strife
And weeping over the Web of Life

To The Accuser Who is The God of This World

Truly My Satan thou art but a Dunce
And dost not know the Garment from the Man
Every Harlot was a Virgin once
Nor canst thou ever change Kate into Nan

Tho' thou art Worship'd by the Names Divine
Of Jesus & Jehovah: thou art still
The Son of Morn in weary Night's decline
The lost Traveller's Dream under the Hill

WILLIAM BLAKE

(*Note.* The reading of the penultimate line given in the Keynes Nonesuch edition is, 'The Son of Man'; but 'Morn' is certainly the word in the British Museum (Carthew) copy.)

I

THE GATES OF PARADISE

THE GATES OF PARADISE is the name Blake gave to a picture-book of engraved plates. This sequence of pictures contains many of Blake's most fundamental ideas and is meant as a record of his experience, and as a guide and commentary for others. The first version of *The Gates of Paradise* was engraved in 1793 and contained sixteen plates and a frontispiece, but it had no text other than the inscriptions (or captions) to the pictures. To the second version, done about the year 1818, he added explanatory couplets entitled *The Keys of the Gates*, together with a prologue and an epilogue, which has an additional illustration (Fig. 19). It is this second version which is reproduced and discussed here.

Blake tended to express himself either in a very concise and epigrammatic form, in aphorisms or lyric poems, or else in a very diffuse manner, as in the Prophetic Books. This picture-book is of the former kind, and since it is very representative of his thought (as indicated by the widely separated dates of the two versions), it makes a useful structure in accordance with which to view the images and symbols of his art. For this reason I have used the sequence of illustrations of this picture-book as a thread on which to string a number of his other important pictures. By this means we can refer them to Blake's own terms of reference, which can be further amplified by quotations from his writings, especially the Prophetic Books and the lyrical poems.

Blake's picture-book is, of course, not the only one of its kind. This means of communication has often been used before. For instance, Francis Quarles's 'Divine Emblems' was extremely popular in the seventeenth century, though the value of its contents is certainly not of a high order from any point of view. The Alchemists in particular were much given to this form of expression. There is the 'Mutus Liber', with pictures only as the name implies, first engraved in 1678 and incorporated in the Geneva edition of the 'Bibliotheca Chemica Curiosa' (1702). The 'Book of Lambspring', which uses pictures and verses, as here, is an extremely interesting and inspiring little treatise; it can be found printed in the 'Hermetic Museum'.[1] By combining the visual image with that of language a most forceful means of communication is made possible, of great significance with regard to psychological and religious experiences.

In *The Gates of Paradise* the eighteen pictures, which compose the sequence, are each in themselves simple and unadorned. They are stark pictorial images. The inscriptions (or captions) and the accompanying verses are also cryptic and at first sight may appear arbitrary and paradoxical. But the purpose of this form of communication is not to make explicit statements. It is to evoke and direct attention to psychological events and states of consciousness by means other than that of the intellectual concept, which is rooted in dualism. Here, the meaning lies implicit in the symbol-image, as it does in any true work of art. Moreover, the pictorial image and the poetic image conveyed by the written word are complementary to one another; in different media they make evocative statements indicative of a common meaning.

Now the image or symbol is not an inferior means of expression, nor is it largely subjective and arbitrary, as it is still far too generally regarded by art critics, art historians, and literary critics. On the contrary, the power of apprehending archetypal symbols and images springs from one of man's most precious faculties, his intuitive faculty. It is on this faculty, above all, that he must rely for perceiving the truth about actual living experience; man can never know the truth about himself, nor find in his relationships with the world that truth or reality which transcends them, unless he develops his

[1] *The Hermetic Museum, restored and enlarged; from the Latin, published in Frankfurt, 1678.* Edited by A. E. Waite, 1893, 2 vols.

power of intuition. The intuitive imagination, which works through symbols, is the very essence of art.[1]

But because the image or symbol speaks not only to man's conscious, thinking side, but also to his unconscious, it is a difficult language. Many people shrink from it in misgiving and fear. Others are so attracted and overwhelmed by it that relationship with other means of cognition is abandoned, and so a vital balance and sense of discrimination is lost. This language of archetypal symbols and images enlists and stirs both sides of man's nature; and because it speaks to the whole man with the many different voices of his complex being, it has to be experienced rather than understood.

The implication of this is that we must first and foremost try to see and feel the living principles about which Blake is speaking in his art. This means that the image or symbol has to be taken inside oneself and understood intuitively, for it is only in this way that it can come to life. The aim of Blake's art is to open the inner world to all those who care to look. He has extraordinary things to show, because he himself saw so far, and so clearly; also because he could bear to look equally on the ugly, the petty, the deformed, and on the free and beautiful.

FRONTISPIECE

Blake's picture-book begins with five introductory couplets (Fig. 1). Opposite this is a frontispiece (Fig. 2) and we must first direct our attention to this, for Blake obviously intends this cryptic pictorial image as a challenge to the reader. We must look carefully into its meaning, as it indicates Blake's attitude to the basic problems of man's life and the possibility of their successful solution; that is, to the problems to which this little book is dedicated.

The frontispiece shows two leaves sprouting from a stalk (Fig. 2); on one climbs a caterpillar, on the other lies a chrysalis with a

[1] This is discussed further in Chapter III.

human child's face. Beneath is written as title to the picture, *What is Man!*, and under this is inscribed a couplet:

The Sun's Light when he unfolds it
Depends on the Organ that beholds it.

What is man? Blake is trying to show that human life lies between two widely separate poles of possibility. Like an insect, which is transformed in the chrysalis from caterpillar to butterfly, so man contains within himself many different levels of potentiality, which may or may not be realized. Will he remain as a crawling thing, like the caterpillar? Or will he awaken to the immeasurable life that can be his, free himself, and become like the butterfly which flies gaily in the sun among the flowers? This is the challenge which Blake throws out at the starting-point of his book, for it is the challenge of life which faces every individual. On the title-page Blake inscribed his book: 'To the Sexes', that is, to every individual who is struggling in life, aware of good and bad, of desire and frustration.

The symbol of the butterfly to represent man's latent possibilities is a very old one. From 'psyche', the Greek word for butterfly, come the many words in our language connected with the idea of the animating principle of life, the soul, the spirit.[1] The symbol is apt because of the extraordinary contrast between the different stages of development in the life cycle of the insect. Similarly human life seems to include widely contrasting states or levels of being; the gamut stretches from the ordinary man-in-the-street to the intellectual or artistic genius; from the savage or simpleton to the enlightened man or saint. But whilst the insect's life develops through its stages in a natural order, this is not so with man.

The Sun's Light . . . depends on the Organ that beholds it. In the natural world the physical sun lights, warms, and fructifies with its

[1] See *Standard Dictionary of Folklore, Mythology and Legend* (Funk and Wagnall, New York, 1950). This was a favourite simile used by P. D. Ouspensky in his oral teaching, though it does not occur in his published introductory lectures, *The Psychology of Man's Possible Evolution* (Hodder and Stoughton, 1951). See also H. G. Baynes, *Mythology of the Soul* (Baillière, Tindall and Cox, 1940), pp. 350, 553 and note.

energy organic life in all its multiplicity, every organism responding and developing according to its kind. Man's case is different: for him it is much more a psychological or spiritual problem. The *Organ* in this case is individual man himself; as he thinks, feels, and acts, that is, as he himself is, such will be his view of life:

> This life's dim Windows of the Soul
> Distorts the Heavens from Pole to Pole
> And leads you to believe a lie
> When you see with, not thro' the eye
> That was born in a night to perish in a night
> When the soul slept in the beams of light.[1]

Seeing with and not through the eyes is for man to rely exclusively on the sense organs for his picture of the world, and by implication to limit himself unduly and restrict his field of consciousness.

The problem of seeing aright is the psychological problem of self-knowledge:

> If the doors of perception were cleansed everything would appear to man as it is, infinite.
>
> For man has closed himself up, till he sees all things through the narrow chinks of his cavern.[2]

This is a fundamental point of view with Blake and it is important to stress this at the outset. The psychological problem of man's nature, what he is, what confines and limits him and so prevents him from realizing his potential vision of the infinite—this is the theme of *The Gates of Paradise*, as indeed it is of all Blake's creative effort in painting and poetry.

There are two pictures by Blake which illustrate very forcibly this contrast between man as he might be, and man as he all too often is (Figs. 20 and 21). 'Glad Day', or 'Albion Rose' (Fig. 20), is one of his best-known designs. The engraving bears the date 1780 (when Blake was aged twenty-three), but this seems to refer to the

[1] Lines from *The Everlasting Gospel* (written about 1818). *The Writings of William Blake*, edited in 3 vols. by Geoffrey Keynes (The Nonesuch Press, London 1925), vol. iii, p. 330. *The Lyrical Poems of William Blake*, edited by John Sampson (Oxford, 1905, &c.), p. 115.

[2] Lines from *The Marriage of Heaven and Hell*, plate 14. See Geoffrey Keynes edition, vol. i, p. 189.

original design, whilst the engraving illustrated probably dates from about 1794–6. Two coloured versions of about the same date are also known.[1] The design shows a young man radiant with life; his posture expresses his joy in his being and his acceptance of it in its fullness. His left foot is on the caterpillar-worm, the constricted state from which he has risen, and behind him a moth or bat-like creature flies away.

Now Blake in his Prophetic Books used two ideas, or images, for measuring man's growth, his limitation to or freedom from the confined and crawling state typified by the caterpillar or worm. Both ideas are expressed in terms of a scale of degrees between two opposite states, or qualities. The first is the scale of Contraction–Expansion; the second is the scale of Opaqueness–Lucidity. In *The Four Zoas*, *Milton*, and *Jerusalem* Blake often uses and refers to these very significant ideas.[2] In the scale of Contraction–Expansion, contraction is the lower limit of the scale; this is a physical, animal-like state which is regulated absolutely by the five senses. This he called the state of Adam. Adam is man, or human nature, dominated and ruled exclusively by physical urges and impulses.

In the scale of Opaqueness–Lucidity, opaqueness stands at the lower limit. This is a state in which all imagination and sensibility, all those promptings of the heart, all understanding which springs from human feeling and sympathy are absent. In this state man is utterly opaque and dark; he is bereft of every glimmer of intuitive insight. This state Blake called Satan.

I shall refer to these two limits, Adam (contraction) and Satan (opaqueness), again when we come to look at his two pictures in *The Gates of Paradise* series which illustrate his ideas of Death as a psychological state (Figs. 13 and 14, which are numbers 11 and 12 of the series). But here, in 'Glad Day', we are concerned with the upper limits of the two scales, with Expansion and Lucidity.

[1] The engraving illustrated (Fig. 3) is at the British Museum (Print Room, Box 1, 1894–6–12–27). See Geoffrey Keynes, *Blake's Engravings: the Separate Plates* (Dublin, 1956), no. ii, 'The Dance of Albion', pp. 6–9. A summary of the studies which have been made of this design is there given, with bibliography.

[2] See, for example, *The Four Zoas*, book 4, lines 269–72; *Milton*, plate 14, lines 20–21; plate 31, lines 35–39. Compare plate 9, lines 30–35; plate 30, lines 29–43; *Jerusalem*, plate 35, lines 1–2; plate 42, lines 29–36; plate 55, lines 36–46.

The idea of Expansion is not so much the full development of man's nature, his faculties and talents, as it is the awareness that he is part of a greater whole; that although he constitutes an individual centre with marvellous capacities, man is not thereby the lord of the earth, nor anything in himself alone. The idea that this individual centre is related to a greater centre, and that ultimately man's powers and very life depend on this realization—this is what is vital in the idea of Expansion. In the coloured versions of 'Glad Day', such as the one at the British Museum, this is vividly expressed in the colours. It is a remarkable experience to study one of these original water-colours. Extraordinary joyousness, fullness, and liberation are expressed in the flashing, multi-coloured aura which surrounds the man. Also expressed there, in the play of colour-tones, and in the contrasts between the deep and dark colours of the earth and lower sky, and the light which is centred round the man's head, is the idea of lucidity. For lucidity refers to man's inner nature, his psychological state, his intuitive awareness of himself, his motives and values. Just as expansion is not primarily concerned with the development of faculties and talents, but the relation with the whole, so lucidity is less concerned with a particular understanding or realization than with awareness of man's total psychosomatic being, with all its contradictions and conflicts. In the state of lucidity the power of control is not egocentric, it is not the usurped tyranny of the head or the heart, nor of the bodily instinctive life; it is something new which springs from integration, something indefinable which Blake hints at and points to in many different ways. 'The Human Imagination, which is the Divine Vision and fruition, in which man liveth eternally' is one way in which he expresses it in 'Milton'.[1]

The engraving of 'Glad Day', or 'Albion Rose' (as it should more properly be called), has the following inscription engraved beneath the design:

> Albion rose from where he laboured at the Mill with slaves,
> Giving himself to the Nations he danced the dance of Eternal Death.[2]

[1] *Milton*, plate 35, lines 19–20.

[2] This inscription is engraved beneath the design in the example belonging to the Lessing

Albion is Blake's name for the human archetype, the Great Man of whom every human being is a part. Albion is the Cosmic Man, the 'Eternal Great Humanity Divine', whose role is played out on earth by every individualized fraction of the living Everyman. Every human life is part of Albion and can realize more or less of the Cosmic Man's total nature; so, too, Albion suffers and triumphs in each individual, as is described in the Prophetic Book, 'Jerusalem'.[1] 'Labouring at the Mill with slaves' means caught in the round of existence, a slave to outer and inner compulsion and consequent conflict. 'The Dance of Eternal Death' is his name for the passage through, and the struggle with, the state of experience. Many names and phrases have been used to allude to this, in mythology and religious literature. It is the 'travail in the murkness', 'the dark night of the soul', Jonah's three-day sojourn in the belly of the whale, the myth of the Nekya, the night journey under or over the sea—all these metaphors and images express the same cardinal idea.[2] Man has to face his own individual nature and experience it in all its darkness and bitterness completely. The god who is sunk and lost in his own Maya can only regain his enlightened state by thoroughly knowing and understanding the mists of Maya.[3] This is the only way back to the light, the only way towards expansion and lucidity.

The main story of his Prophetic Book, 'Milton', is based on this fundamental mythological symbol. 'I go to Eternal Death', says

J. Rosenwald collection, National Gallery, Washington, D.C.; the British Museum example has been cut down but remains of the inscription can be seen. See Geoffrey Keynes, op. cit. 'Albion Rose' seems to me a much more suitable title than 'The Dance of Albion', as it is the moment of his arising from servitude which is shown.

[1] The phrase quoted comes from *Milton*, plate 2, line 8. The Albion myth, or symbol, is used throughout all Blake's later work. Compare 'Adam Kadmon' of the Kabbala, and 'Narayana' the Cosmic Man, and manifestation of Vishnu, of Indian mythology. For more about Albion, see pp. 22 and 65, and *Notes A* and *F* (pp. 128–9).

[2] These phrases are taken from *The Scale of Perfection*, a fourteenth-century text attributed to Walter Hilton (J. M. Watkins, 1923); St. John of the Cross; Matt. xii. 40, &c. The theme of the Nekya is extensively treated in Jungian literature. See C. G. Jung, *Psychology of the Unconscious* (Routledge and Kegan Paul, 1919), pp. 131–2 (quoting Frobenius); H. G. Baynes, op. cit., pp. 425, 441, &c.

[3] See Heinrich Zimmer, *Myths and Symbols in Indian Art and Civilisation* (Bollingen Foundation, Washington, 1946). Sri Ramakrishna said that even God gets lost in his own Maya; for his sayings about Maya, see *The Gospel of Ramakrishna* (Sri Ramakrishna Math, Madras, 1947), pp. 180, 199, &c.

Milton, as he prepares to descend again into the world to redeem his unresolved conflicts and problems.[1] Moreover, this facing up to life in all its darkness, conflict, and horror, as well as in its beautiful and benign aspect, is a service not only to the individual, but also to humanity at large. 'Giving himself to the Nations, he danced the dance of Eternal Death.' Blake has stated his point of view about this very forcibly and very clearly in a short poem called 'The Grey Monk'; he used a shortened form of this for the prologue to chapter three of his last great Prophetic Book, 'Jerusalem'. He states the case there for the principle of action in non-action. The fundamentally important thing is to live one's life fully and deeply as one believes in it; a life that is true and right in itself is a tremendous spiritual force though it may appear inglorious, impotent, and even indifferent to the world's great wrongs:

For a Tear is an intellectual thing
And a sigh is the Sword of an Angel King
And the bitter groan of a Martyr's woe
Is an arrow from the Almightie's bow.

Blake's life itself is one of the great vindications of this conviction. Although he was almost completely unknown, disregarded, and frequently ridiculed in his own lifetime and for many years after his death, his influence on later generations has steadily strengthened and widened, until now, two hundred years after his birth, we are gradually awakening to his true significance as artist, poet, and seer.

The above exposition of 'Glad Day', and its relation with Blake's thought, has been rather lengthy, but all the ideas referred to play an important part in *The Gates of Paradise* sequence and we shall meet them again.

There is now the opposite pole of human possibility to consider, the man who remains as a crawling thing, or worm. One of Blake's illustrations to Young's 'Night Thoughts' shows this state (Fig. 21); it depicts an old man who has remained like a crawling worm.[2] He is bound by a chain ('in chains of the mind locked up')[3] and the

[1] *Milton*, plate 15, line 14 (illustrated on plate 16; or plate 13 of the British Museum copy).
[2] Young's *Night Thoughts*, book 1, p. 12.
[3] Quoted from *Milton*, plate 3, line 6. Compare *The Four Zoas*, book 4, lines 211–14.

mirror which he holds before him reflects nothing beyond the narrow horizon of his own restricted thought. This is the all-too-common man, 'a worm seventy inches long', to use a favourite phrase of Blake's.[1] A pungent epigram written by Blake, about the painter Thomas Stothard, with whom he quarrelled over the 'Canterbury Pilgrims' picture, is a useful comment on this phrase. The epigram, written in Blake's private note-book, gives caustic expression to what he thought about this sort of level of humanity:

> S (Stothart) in Childhood on the Nursery floor
> Was extreme Old and most extremely poor.
> He is grown old and rich and what he will:—
> He is extreme old and extreme poor still.[2]

PROLOGUE

After the frontispiece there follows a prologue of five couplets, which is without illustrations (Fig. 1). This prologue provides a key to the theme of the book and it is important to emphasize the ideas it contains. I shall try to elucidate these ideas with the help of six illustrations taken from elsewhere in his work, where their terms of reference can be more amply studied.

To begin with the first two couplets, which read:

> *Mutual Forgiveness of each Vice*
> *Such are the Gates of Paradise*
> *Against the Accuser's chief desire*
> *Who walked among the Stones of Fire.*

Forgiveness is stressed as the cardinal principle. But as Blake insists throughout his writing, forgiveness does not only apply to others, but first and foremost to ourselves, our own faults, failures, and vices. We have first to learn to know and accept ourselves as we

[1] *Jerusalem*, plate 33, lines 5–6.

[2] Geoffrey Keynes edition, vol. iii, p. 58. That this stricture on his old friend Stothard may be exaggerated or ill justified is not here relevant.

are. The idea of *mutual forgiveness*, of acceptance and understanding, is set off against that of accusation, *the Accuser*. Let us look first at illustrations of the Accuser. There is an engraving of 'The Accusers' of theft, murder, and adultery designed in about 1793; the illustration given here (Fig. 22) is taken from the British Museum example, which dates from about 1810. Now what do these three figures suggest? Certainly this is not a commonplace view of accusation; it is not the straightforward accusation of a knowing wrongdoer. Nor are these three accusers opposing a point of view with which they cannot agree in an honest and direct manner. They suggest, in fact, the opposite of understanding and acceptance. Blake has made them appear supercilious, spiteful, fearful, and uncertain of themselves. They are hypocrites. They are themselves guilty of hidden but racking desires, which they have outwardly suppressed, but which in their act of accusation they are projecting on to others. The venom of their attitude comes from their own frustrated wills. They are blind to the true nature of their own inner impulses. They are, in their state of biting conflict, looking for the scapegoat. That is the secret motive of their accusation, which is the opposite of understanding and acceptance.

But what does it mean—the Accuser *who walked among the Stones of Fire*? This phrase is a reference to a passage in Ezekiel (chap. xxviii), where the expressions 'the Covering Cherub' and 'the Stones of Fire' occur.[1] Blake took many of his symbols from the Bible, or rather he borrowed names and images from Bible contexts to serve him as symbols; in this way the wider terms of reference of the Bible texts would help to elucidate and colour his own particular record of experiences. He used the expression, 'the Covering Cherub', as a name for a psychological state or value. The Covering Cherub, in Blake's language, denotes the principle of

[1] 'Thou art the anointed cherub that covereth; and I have set thee so: thou wast upon the holy mountain of God; thou hast walked up and down in the midst of the stones of fire.' '. . . and I will destroy thee, O covering cherub, from the midst of the stones of fire.' (Ezek. xxviii. 14, 16.) For the engraved and coloured versions of The Accusers, see Geoffrey Keynes, *Blake's Engravings: the Separate Plates*, no. vii, pp. 19–22. The third engraved version, used here, is inscribed: 'The Accusers of (Theft, Adultery, Murder, A Scene in the last judgement) Satan's Holy Trinity, The Accuser, The Judge, The Executioner.'

ethical judgement; on this the development and organization of a civilized society in great measure depends. It is a psychological value which guards over mankind in his social and cultural capacity, just as the Cherubs guarded over the Ark of the Covenant of the Israelites (token of their union with and submission to the Deity). In the passage in Ezekiel it is the King of Tyre who is referred to as a Covering Cherub, because he had excelled as a successful leader and protagonist of civilization and culture; but Ezekiel is now taking him to task on other scores. It is from this context that Blake adopted the expression 'Covering Cherub'. The *Stones of Fire* refer to the force or energy which resides in this ethical impulse. The fire and zeal of social improvement, and efforts for the good of the community, can easily become tainted with personal ambition. The drive inherent in the political or national leader derives from this source, but can lead also to the tyrant and the despot. So too, on a more personal level, the drive behind the pseudo-saint and the ascetic often has its roots in this same fire. The fire of the inquisition and of all persecution in the name of truth and goodness shows its flagrant distortion.

For the Covering Cherub, as a psychological value, is extremely prone to become inflated with egotism and self-esteem, and so by over-evaluation to become a hindrance and an evil and thus to fall from its rightful station. Then he becomes a tyrant, swollen with self-righteous pride. He becomes the Accuser with his ever-narrowing moral law, the puritan, the inquisitor, the liquidator of deviational views. The link between the Covering Cherub and the Accuser is an ever-present one; when the energy of the former inflates the ego and causes it to assume the role of the tyrant, it becomes the Accuser.

Illustrated in Figure 23 is a representation of the Covering Cherub; it is a water-colour in the Tate Gallery.[1] This picture is often known as 'Lucifer in his former Glory', and it is true that the

[1] The passage from Ezekiel quoted above, referring to the 'covering cherub' (verses 12–16), was inscribed upon the mount. See *The Blake Collection of W. Graham Robertson*, edited and introduced by Kerrison Preston (Faber and Faber, 1952), pp. 60–61. Originally in Thomas Butts's collection.

idea of Lucifer and of the Covering Cherub are not very far apart. He is shown in his splendour, equipped with great power and with ministers to execute his will and designs. But he is shown on the very verge of his fall. The dangers of accusation and condemnation, although closely linked with the ethical principle which is such a fundamental part of human nature, are nevertheless a great stumbling-block in the path of understanding and acceptance, that is, of Forgiveness, which as Blake asserts is the very threshold of paradise.

Now to conclude the prologue, there are the three following couplets:

Jehovah's Finger Wrote the Law
Then Wept: then rose in Zeal & Awe
And in the midst of Sinai's heat
Hid it beneath his Mercy Seat
O Christians Christians! tell me Why
You rear it on your Altars high.

Here Blake says that a code of moral law springs from what we may call man's higher nature. But higher still, the moral law is hidden in mercy. Man has to go beyond the moral law.

The debased, dead letter of the law is an obstacle against which Blake was always vehement, and he was tireless in pointing to its more hidden and subtle forms. In his Prophetic Book, 'America', he depicted the image of authority, the dead letter of the law, in a design which is illustrated here (Fig. 26).[1] He there called it the 'Stone of Night', for it is a rock or stone which blocks further development. In his 'Illustrations of the Book of Job', a sequence of twenty-one engravings with texts commenting on the Biblical story of Job, he is much concerned with the connexion between the authoritarian moral code based on rigid concepts of right and wrong, and the harmful effects which arise from accusation and condemnation. Plate 10 of the Job series (see Fig. 24) shows Job's three friends who have come to comfort him, but who appear in the

[1] *America*, plate 10 (Fitzwilliam Museum, Riches copy).

guise of his accusers. These friends are sure that the misfortunes which have befallen Job must in some way be due to his secret sins, his failure to live up to the moral standard. They are convinced that his trouble springs from his guilt, and their message, which they make plain to Job, is one of accusation. But in fact, as Blake interprets the story and as he subtly conveys in the sequel, Job's trouble lay in exactly the reverse direction. Job's moral efforts, his rigid adherence to a code, his self-righteousness, and his consequent lack of true insight and humanity, had led him into a deep and devastating conflict with his own nature. This (in essence) is Blake's interpretation of the Job story.[1]

The principle on which Blake insists is quite otherwise: *Mutual Forgiveness of each Vice*. But for this to come about there must be a psychological revolution, a turning about at the centre. There is a very remarkable illustration of this process in 'Milton' (Fig. 25).[2] The poet Milton, whom Blake in his Prophetic Book brought back to earth to redeem his puritanical intransigence, finally realizes that this is only done by self-observation and inner awareness. He realizes that the false tyrant in himself must be dethroned, call this tyrant by what name you will—the Accuser, the self or Selfhood, the ego or ego-personality, the super-ego, father figure, image of the Wise Old Man. But in so far as any of these aspects of the false centre is seen for what it is, to this extent it is immediately dethroned. In his notes on 'A Vision of the last Judgment' Blake has given a clear exposition of the principle that, if error is once seen for what it is, then it can be cast out, or transcended. Here, in 'Milton', we are shown this fundamental revolution as it concerns the selfhood. Beneath the picture a line of the text serves as an inscription: 'To Annihilate the Self-hood of Deceit and False Forgiveness.'

In 'Jerusalem' this same idea is put in another way. Albion, the now fallen, degenerate Everyman of England, is moralizing, analysing, accusing human nature of sin and vice, threatening it with

[1] See J. H. Wicksteed, *Blake's Vision of the Book of Job* (1910), and the briefer commentary in S. Foster Damon, *William Blake, his philosophy and symbols* (New York, 1924, reprinted 1947), chap. 30.

[2] *Milton*, plate 15 (British Museum copy).

punishment. Then Jerusalem—who stands for man's inner voice, his soul-figure, his anima—speaks:

> Jerusalem then stretch'd her hand toward the Moon and spoke:
> Why should Punishment Weave the Veil with Iron Wheels of War
> When Forgiveness might it Weave with Wings of Cherubim?

These lines are illustrated with a picture (Fig. 27).[1] This is one of the comparatively rare instances of an illustration to Blake's text which corresponds rather exactly with the verbal image. For Blake was never content to illustrate his text in an obvious, superficial manner. He had as it were two eyes, an eye for the verbal image as it is spoken and written, and an eye for the pictorial image. The inner truth that he apprehended was something other than either of these, not confined or explicit in either of them, but something which could be expressed or implied by their means. For truth, reality, is always beyond the formulation both of words and of pictorial images. Sometimes the pictorial symbol parallels or amplifies the written one; sometimes it gives the contrasting aspect, or opposite and contrary point of view. But always this double mode of expression is focused on man's subtle and complex nature, his illusions, self-deceptions, conceits, and his contradictory and insatiable desires. This twofold artistic capacity, and his vision of the infinite which the coarseness and opaqueness of human nature unnecessarily obscures, makes the creative work of Blake in art and poetry such an incomparable source of wisdom.

MAIN SEQUENCE OF PICTURES

We now come to the main sequence of pictures. There are sixteen pictures in *The Gates of Paradise*, besides a frontispiece and tailpiece, and they are numbered in sequence by Blake. Each picture has a brief inscription or caption, and each has one or more couplets of commentary; these couplets, which compose the text, are called *The Keys of the Gates* and have numbers beside them corresponding

[1] *Jerusalem*, plate 22.

with their respective pictures. I shall make my references to these clear, as we proceed, so that further designs and quotations from Blake's other works, which I shall introduce for the sake of elucidation and comparison, can always be kept distinct from them without any possible confusion.

PICTURE 1. The child-mandrake (Fig. 3). The inscription reads: *I found him beneath a Tree.* Two couplets of the text refer to this picture:

My Eternal Man set in Repose
The Female from his darkness rose
And She found me beneath a Tree
A Mandrake & in her Veil hid me.

This picture stresses the physical, biological aspect of man. It emphasizes that man grows up powerfully conditioned by his mother, his inherited human nature, and his childhood years.

The mandrake is mentioned a number of times in the Old Testament and the reference is to a root used as an aphrodisiac. In the well-known story of Genesis, Leah, Jacob's first wife, was in rivalry with Rachel, his second and favourite wife.[1] Leah tried to compete with Rachel for Jacob's affections by this means and sent her son Reuben to gather mandrake roots. Blake, with this and perhaps other Biblical references in mind, is here asserting the powerful part played in man's nature by sex, and that man and woman spring from the sexual process. This is a fundamental part of man's nature which cannot be thought away or ignored.

The Tree, in this picture, stands for the ancestral line from which the child springs. This ancestry includes his family lineage, his social group, and his wider biological inheritance. The child is born under the shadow of this Tree.[2]

He is nurtured by his mother. The veil in which she hides him is his inherited nature, the instinctive side of life, in which as a child he is contained in a relatively undifferentiated state. Later, in adult years, with the growth of individual consciousness, he will

[1] Gen. xxx. 14–17.
[2] For tree symbolism, see H. G. Baynes, op. cit., pp. 434–5, 499, &c.

begin to revolt and come into conflict with this conditioned existence in his effort to free himself from it.

The undifferentiated, instinctive side of life, which links man with his inherited past, the race and the animal kingdom, is always referred to by Blake as feminine. This, indeed, is how it is normally apprehended in image-language, in visions, dreams, and myths. It is the equivalent of the Yin of Chinese philosophy, that is, the conditioned as opposed to the conditioning, the receptive in contrast to the creative. In Hindu philosophy it is the female Shakti, the counterpart of the male Shiva. This equivalence is found in a thousand different forms as the female goddess throughout the world's mythology. In Jung's analytical psychology this is recognized in the manifestations of the dark and light anima.

Now, in the situation alluded to in the picture, a problem is stated which Blake realized to be fundamental. It is the seeming conflict of the light and dark aspects of life, of the formative or creative and the conditioned or receptive, of God and Nature, spiritual man and natural man, generation and regeneration. This problem faces every adolescent as development and differentiation take place, and as he becomes aware of the opposite and contradictory elements in his make-up. In one of the 'Songs of Experience', 'To Tirzah', Blake has obviously been deeply concerned with this problem and has given us his poetic statement about it:

> Thou Mother of my mortal part
> With cruelty didst mold my heart
> And with false self-deceiving tears
> Didst bind my nostrils, eyes and ears.

But there is a possibility of liberation from this conditioned state. On one of the figures in the illustration which accompanies this poem is written: 'It is raised a spiritual body'; and the poem concludes with the line, addressed to the female principle: 'Then what have I to do with thee?' For it is Blake's view that man is only bound by the instinctive, natural man (personified as Tirzah) so long as he takes this part to be the whole. The natural man certainly exists, but it is only a partial, one-sided aspect of the total man. In the discovery of this lies the possible solution of the problem.

That is the meaning of the rather enigmatic first couplet of *The Keys of the Gates*:

> *My Eternal Man set in Repose*
> *The Female from his darkness rose.*

Man is part of the 'Divine Humanity', the 'Eternal Great Humanity' (in Blake's phrase).[1] In Reality, in Eternity, in the true state which far transcends man's ordinary limited concepts, that other part of him is sleeping. His totality, including that 'sleeping' part of him in which he is united with the Divine, is however always there in potentiality. This is the 'Real Human' which has to be awakened.[2] Because this other side of him is sleeping, because he has lost or abandoned his wholeness, the Female rises from his darkness to dominate him. The more he mistakes the part for the whole the greater is her domination. This idea is expressed by Blake in the myth of the sleeping Albion, which runs through all his later works.[3] It is a mythological image, or symbol, which entirely transcends the bald statement of it I have given here, but in Blake's hands it is an instrument of infinite subtlety and suggestiveness.[4]

The Female who rises from man's darkness is natural life dominated by the five senses, orientated almost exclusively to sense perception, and looking outwards. This interpretation of the myth of the temptation and fall of Eve is portrayed in a tempera painting from the Stirling Collection, now in the Victoria and Albert Museum (Fig. 29). Adam, the male, formative aspect of life, has fallen asleep beside the River of Paradise; he is the *Eternal Man set in Repose.* The sun, which here represents the light of inner

[1] For example: *Vision of the Last Judgment*: 'the Eternal Births of Intellect from the Divine Humanity' (Keynes edition, vol. iii, p. 157); 'All springing from the Divine Humanity . . . He is the Bread and Wine; he is the Water of Life' (ibid., p. 156). *Milton*, plate 33, lines 15, 17: 'Lo, the Eternal Great Humanity . . . Walks among all his awful Family seen in every face.' *Jerusalem*, plate 15, lines 6–7: 'I see the Four-fold Man, The Humanity in deadly sleep, And its fallen Emanation.'

[2] *Milton*, plate 22, line 13: 'His real Human walked above.'

[3] See *Note A*, p. 128.

[4] See *Note B*, p. 128.

awareness, is in eclipse. Eve, the Female, that is, the conditioned, instinctive aspect of man's nature, then assumes control. This partial aspect of him is open to temptation, to mistake, to misunderstanding. The serpent towers over Eve and deceives her.

But what is the significance of the serpent? As with all vital and powerfully felt symbols, the serpent-symbol contains within itself its own opposite. This is what makes symbols so puzzling and refractory to intellectual study, whilst intuitive imagination works with them freely, for they are a unique instrument of communication.

The serpent is primarily the symbol of the infinite locked up in the finite; the image of the misconception of the part as the whole. The finite thinks it can contain and comprehend the infinite, the part the whole. So long as there is this thought, this misconception, the serpent is the subtle deceiver. Or stated in kinetic psychological terms, the libido or life-energy is the great tempter.

Blake illustrated the title-page of his Prophetic Book 'Europe' with a magnificent involute serpent (Fig. 28). For in this poem he tried to explain that it was precisely this problem and misconception which was the great source of error and evil in European civilization from the time of Jesus to his own day. On plate 13 of this Prophetic Book[1] he drew another serpent rising in spirals up one margin of the page. On this page he expressed his ideas at some length about this symbol. For example:

> Image of the Infinite shut up in finite revolutions,

and again:

> Thought changed the Infinite to a Serpent.

True, this is only one aspect of the serpent symbol, but it is the dominant one, and that which particularly concerns us here. For the next couplet in our text reads:

> *Serpent Reasonings us entice*
> *Of Good & Evil: Virtue & Vice.*

As the child grows into the adolescent he begins to develop his rational faculty. He begins to see everything in comparative terms

[1] Fitzwilliam Museum, Riches copy.

of good and bad, virtue and vice. For the reason, the intellectual function, is fundamentally dualistic. It opens up the opposites in everything and shows contradiction, conflict, and irreconcilability. Man's conscious and unconscious sides now begin to stand in opposition to one another; hence *Serpent Reasonings* with its dualism.

A few lines later in the text Blake will again take up this division of everything into contraries and opposites, but before this he shows us four pictures representing the Four Elements. For man contains within himself four levels of existence, or four modes of life, which can be represented by the images of the elements, Water, Earth, Air, and Fire.

PICTURE 2. Water. Inscribed: *Thou Waterest him with Tears* (Fig. 4). This element represents the bodily, physical life ruled by the organs of sense perception and the sympathetic nervous system. In Blake's own nomenclature this is 'Tharmas', so often called by him 'Watery Tharmas'.

The Text (half a couplet only) reads:

Doubt Self Jealous Watry folly

The life of sense perception by itself is a source of contradiction and doubt, the self seeking its own but never able to satisfy itself. This is the 'watery shore', a basic image of Blake's, as for example in 'The Bard', and 'Earth's Answer', the two poems usually given first in the 'Songs of Experience'.

PICTURE 3. Earth. Inscribed: *He struggles into life* (Fig. 5). The text (again half a couplet) reads:

Struggling thro Earths Melancholy

The element Earth stands for instinct, leading to intuition, based on the idea of the creative seed hidden in the earth. Usually with Blake the earth is regarded as feminine, the conditioned principle, as for instance in the two poems just cited; it corresponds with Eno in 'The Book of Los', and the 'Shadowy Female' in 'The Four Zoas'.[1]

[1] See Foster Damon's comments on Eno, the 'earth-mother', op. cit., p. 148. Blake's first draft for the opening lines of *The Four Zoas* read: 'This is the Song of the Aged Mother. . . And thus beginneth the Book of Vala' (see Keynes edition, vol. ii, p. 377).

But here Earth is taken in its aspect as one of the Four Elements, and therein a paradox is implied.

The idea expressed in this picture is of the creative seed hidden in the earth, just as it is also hidden in man's feminine, instinctive physical nature. It is through the finite that the infinite is seen. The element Earth is here the counterpart of 'Los', who in Blake's nomenclature is the fallen form of 'Urthona'. Los is the power of intuitive imagination, ultimately of creative and unifying vision. In this last aspect Los again becomes Urthona, which is spirit or reality transcending all forms and distinctions. Therefore Urthona is equally present in the opposite poles of existence, in the receptive as well as the creative, in earth as much as in spirit. This is clearly expressed in the phrase 'Urthona's dens', which Blake uses in that very significant vision of his, recorded in the 'Song of Liberty', as well as elsewhere.[1] Here then is the paradox which sees spirit manifesting in its own opposite, which can be expressed by the idea of the creative seed hidden in the earth. It can also be thought of as the contrary state which is beginning the cycle of revolution which will lead back to that which is its own polar opposite. For this conception of the relativity of contrary states, the identity of the opposites, is fundamental to Blake.[2] Also, it should here be pointed out that Urthona, who represents an altogether transcendental state beyond all human conception, scarcely ever appears in Blake's work except as he is manifested in the world of relative existence as Los.

PICTURE 4. Air. Inscription: *On cloudy Doubts and Reasoning Cares* (Fig. 6). The element Air represents the life of thought and reason, the rational or intellectual faculty. From the intellectual function man obtains all his conceptions of law, system, and order. Since the stars and planets in their motions manifest the laws of Nature on their grandest scale, they are used by Blake in a traditional manner to allude to the rational principle, as in this picture. Stars

[1] *The Song of Liberty* is included in copies of *The Marriage of Heaven and Hell*, at the end; see verse 16. See also, *The Four Zoas*, book 5, line 189. Compare his later expression of this in *Milton*, plate 35, lines 40–41: 'For God himself enters Death's Door always with those that enter And lays down in the Grave with them, in Visions of Eternity.' Blake's images alluded to here correspond with the archetype of the 'Deus Absconditus'.

[2] See *Note C*, p. 128.

surround the thinking man beyond the confines of his cloud. Clouds, which obscure and refract the light, represent the duality of the thinking process, which involves the awareness of comparison and contradiction. From the negative aspect of the thinking function arise doubt and care, fear and shame. For the calculating processes of reason, along with purpose, aim and hope, also bring in their train anxiety and fear. The awareness of contradiction leads not only to doubt and care, but also to feelings of shame. The line of the text reads:

Naked in Air in Shame & Fear.

The nakedness refers to awareness; shame and fear to the negative aspect of dualistic knowledge based on thought. 'Urizen' is Blake's name for the rational, thinking function.

PICTURE 5. Fire. Inscription: *That end in endless Strife* (Fig. 7). The line from the text is:

Blind in Fire with shield & spear.

Fire is the element of the passions, that is, of the feeling and emotional nature of man. It is the source of man's psychological energy, of his desires, efforts, and aspirations. It is the 'hell' which is co-eternal in man with the 'heaven' of law and order (as Blake affirmed in his 'Marriage of Heaven and Hell'). Fire is therefore armed with the spear and shield of psychological, or spiritual, warfare. From the point of view of reason, to which feeling and emotion always stand in opposition, it appears as blind, because it is impulsive and not actuated by calculation and forethought, as reason is. In Blake's nomenclature 'Luvah' is always at war with 'Urizen' (reason).

The Four Elements, thus understood, represent four living principles which man includes in himself. They are four spheres of life in which he participates. When they are not in harmony they subject man to a double, bi-polar tension, which racks him like the figure of a cross.

The 'Four Mighty Ones in every Man' (a phrase taken from 'The Four Zoas'),[1] correspond with the four psychological functions as

[1] See *Note D*, p. 128.

studied in analytical psychology. The correspondence is as follows. Water represents the body, that is, the function of Sensation, Blake's 'Tharmas'; Earth stands for the Intuitive function, Blake's 'Los'; Air for the Thinking function, 'Urizen'; Fire for the Feeling function, 'Luvah'. These four functions, or principles, or 'Living Creatures', are called by Blake the 'Four Zoas'. Their rivalries, combats, deprivations, and distress constitute a large part of Blake's myths as they unfold in the Prophetic Books, especially in 'The Four Zoas'. Needless to say, Blake throughout is only intent on understanding and describing, by means of symbols and images, psychological states and conflicts, and their solution. The understanding of the Four Elements in this symbolic, psychological way is not peculiar to Blake and has a whole tradition behind it, both in Western and Eastern thought.[1]

In 'Milton' Blake has given a very interesting diagram of the Four Zoas (Fig. 30).[2] They are shown related to the four points of the compass, and they contain the egg in which are the two lower limits of the scales mentioned previously, Adam (contraction) and Satan (opacity), as can be seen in the reproduction given here. The diagram also indicates Milton's track as he descends again into human existence, terminating near the point marked Adam. This is a diagram of the exploration which every man, who is intent on following his experience to the end, must pursue in order to gain a clear insight into his own nature. It is a diagram of a fundamental aspect of man's nature, of his 'Eternal lineaments', as Blake named it.[3]

The four lines of *The Keys of the Gates,* which comment on the four pictures of the Elements, are followed by two couplets which relate further to this fourfold division of man's nature, and the stresses between them. For, as the child grows up and develops his faculties, he becomes aware of contrary forces and seemingly irreconcilable drives and urges. He has already begun to develop the

[1] For the symbolic theme of the Four Elements, see the present author's *Meaning and Symbol in three modern Artists* (Faber and Faber, 1955), pp. 130–4.

[2] *Milton,* plate 32 (British Museum copy).

[3] 'Judge then of thy Own Self: thy Eternal lineaments explore What is Eternal and what Changeable, and what Annihilable.' *Milton,* plate 35, lines 30–31.

conscious control which emanates from his ego-personality, and he has begun to experience the consequent struggles. Entering on the state of manhood he becomes keenly alive to these stresses and tensions:

> *Two Horn'd Reasoning Cloven Fiction*
> *In Doubt which is Self contradiction*
> *A dark Hermaphrodite I stood*
> *Rational Truth Root of Evil & Good.*

Human nature is now at war within itself. The rational functions seem to contradict and belie the irrational ones; consciousness finds itself in opposition to the unconscious. It is a state which Blake calls a *dark Hermaphrodite*, that is a state divided between two unreconciled centres of value and action.

The conscious, or rational functions, championed by reason, oppress and resist the irrational unconscious functions.[1] The masculine, formative, light side of life, instead of receiving and integrating the dark feminine side, opposes it and tries to overpower and dominate it.

One of Blake's colour prints known as 'Satan exulting over Eve' (Fig. 31)[2] refers to this situation. Consciousness identifies itself with the ego, the selfhood. It knows no other values, no other light. It is God, and will tolerate nothing beside itself. It becomes Satan. The serpent, which is the part which proudly conceives itself to be the whole, the finite which has forgotten the infinite, coils round Eve, the female principle, triumphing over her, binding her, repressing and suppressing. The psychological meaning of this is conveyed with extraordinary intensity in Blake's picture.

This is one aspect of the *dark Hermaphrodite*. But we must not forget the opposite aspect of the hermaphroditic state. This is depicted in plate 75 of 'Jerusalem' as the Dragon-females (Fig. 32). In this case, the unconscious predominates over consciousness, but in the form of a displaced affect (to use this word in its psychological

[1] For the classification of psychological functions as rational and irrational, see C. G. Jung, *Psychological Types* (Routledge and Kegan Paul, 1923), chapters 10 and 11.

[2] In the possession of Mr. Gregory Bateson (U.S.A.).

sense). For the unconscious can erupt into consciousness not only in more or less obvious ways, such as when passion or hysteria carry a man away against his 'better nature', but also in much more devious and subtle ways. The Dragon-females, as Blake explains in 'Jerusalem', are war masquerading as religion, the plausible exterior which is really driven by a hidden and unrecognized impulse, which dare not be admitted. It is the wolf in sheep's clothing, which honestly believes itself to be a very good sheep, because it has failed to understand and become reconciled to its own nature. This is the worst kind of hypocrisy, or 'opaqueness', from which the most terrible of human evils spring. Every activity based on the rationalization of an affect is an example of this, in greater or less degree. All worldly empires, crusades, and militant ideologies share all too much of this character.

To return to the two couplets, *Rational Truth* sees man's fourfold nature as a mine of evil and good. Its account of human nature is that it is composed of *Evil & Good.* For the intellect by its very nature is dualistic, and as it is only one of the four psychological functions it can by no means solve the problem of human nature by itself; it can never bring enlightenment.

And so the sixth picture of the *Gates of Paradise* series (Fig. 8) is introduced by two couplets:

Round me flew the Flaming Sword
Round her snowy Whirlwinds roard
Freezing her Veil the Mundane Shell
I rent the Veil where the Dead dwell.

The *Flaming Sword* refers to the cutting, dualistic, rational mind, which in this context is in the service of man's moral sense and his desire for perfection. For at this point in *The Gates of Paradise* Blake is visualizing the problem from the point of view of the young aspiring man, desperately concerned with the problem of perfection, of good and evil. But these very intellectual powers and moral qualities in the hands of 'fallen', inharmonious man, keep him from Paradise, like the Angel with the flaming sword stationed at the Gate of Eden.

The snowy whirlwinds are the rationalizations and repressions which bind the unconscious and suppress it, instead of integrating it. This image is found repeatedly used by Blake in connexion with Urizen, particularly in the 'Book of Urizen' and 'The Four Zoas'.[1]

The result of this freezing rationalization and repression is that a *veil*, or semi-opaque barrier, forms between man's conscious and unconscious sides. The veil or semi-opaque obstruction is also called by Blake the *Mundane Shell.*[2] *Freezing her Veil, the Mundane Shell.* As a consequence, man loses contact with the vital source of life; he is no longer open to life as it actually is, either within himself or without. Somehow he becomes divided from the dark feminine aspect of life, though it is a vital component part of himself.

There is an interesting illustration of this image of the *veil* given in plate 12 of 'Europe' (Fig. 33), where it is seen forming like a spider's web over external Nature.[3]

But the veil quickly becomes opaque and solid. It becomes the *Mundane Shell.* This is a favourite image of Blake's and refers to the world as it appears to fallen, divided, rationalistic man. We have already seen this egg with its shell containing Adam and Satan in the diagram of the Four Zoas, showing the path down which Milton had to descend to try to understand himself (Fig. 30). The Mundane Shell is the hard, refractory, illusion of Maya. This brings us to the sixth picture.

PICTURE 6. Child hatching from egg (Fig. 8). This picture indicates the state of man when he first seriously realizes that there is something basically wrong with his view of the world, and that all his efforts have so far only served further to confound and enmesh him. It points to a very important turning-point in life, the moment when the age of experience (which has already long since succeeded the age of innocence) is accepted as such. It is a sort of second birth, the beginning of a reawakening. Like a reborn child—so foreign is the new realization from his erstwhile confident, aspiring, ego-

[1] *Book of Urizen*, chaps. 8 and 9. *The Four Zoas*, book 5, line 107: 'Snows of Urizen'.

[2] See *The Four Zoas*, book 2, lines 19–25. *Milton*, plate 38, lines 24–31, 40–43.

[3] Compare *Jerusalem*, plate 47, line 11: 'And the Veil of Vala is composed of the Spectres of the Dead.'

dominated attitude—he momentarily awakens to the fact that he is irrevocably caught in conflict, doubt, and disharmony. *I rent the Veil where the Dead dwell,* reads the line from the couplet which specifically refers to this picture. For the state of experience, at its first impact, when fully accepted as fact, is like a scene of death. Here there is no assurance, no triumphant and eternal ideal, no absolute standard and measure to which a man can cling. For in this moment of realization the mind-made standards and ideals have to be given up, and the absolute relativity of experience has to be accepted. The contradictory values and desires springing from man's fourfold nature confront him, for one brief moment, with a sense of chaos, helplessness: the abandonment of death.

The rending of the veil where the dead dwell means the facing up to the 'Image of Sin and Death', to use St. Paul's phrase. This experience has been described in a hundred different ways, but always with the emphasis on darkness, death, submergence in the underworld; although out of this very darkness and abandonment to death springs light, the flower of true awakening. For this is the entering into the state of experience in its reality. It is the 'dark night of the soul', or the 'travail in the nought', the 'travail in the murkness' (to use two phrases from English fourteenth-century mystics). It is the 'Night Journey under the sea', a mythological theme of universal recurrence (which has been especially studied by Jungian psychology).[1]

The inscription under this sixth picture reads: *At length for hatching ripe he breaks the shell.* At last he can abandon the petty assurances of his mind-made values, his repressions, and rationalizations, and begin to accept life in its totality, as it really is. Now, before he can find the Gates of Paradise he must willingly and thoroughly explore the 'Caverns of the Grave', and like Thel visit the 'couches of the dead'.[2] He must abandon himself, know himself in all his aspects good and bad, the dark, female, instinctive aspect,

[1] *The Cloud of Unknowing,* edited by Evelyn Underhill (John M. Watkins, 1946); *The Scale of Perfection* (John M. Watkins, 1923). See also p. 12, n. 2.

[2] See Geoffrey Keynes edition, vol. iii, p. 85: 'The Caverns of the Grave I've seen . . .'; for 'the couches of the dead', *The Book of Thel,* plate 4.

as well as the aspiring Apollonian side he had formerly liked to know. There is no other way to become a true human being, a 'Real Human'; all other ways are counterfeits. This is the very core of the human problem; it is always insisted upon by Blake and reiterated in the opening lines of his last and most complete Prophetic Book, 'Jerusalem':

> Of the Sleep of Ulro! and of the passage through
> Eternal Death! and of the awakening to Eternal Life.

This entering into the reality of experience is referred to in the poem 'To Tirzah', already cited, where the expression 'the Sexes' again occurs (compare the title-page of *The Gates of Paradise*):

> The Sexes sprung from Shame and pride
> Blow'd in the morn, in evening died;
> But Mercy chang'd death into Sleep
> The Sexes rose to work and weep.

In other words, man enjoys and suffers many experiences, and because of his complex nature he feels now shame, now pride, and all the other opposites of feeling. But in this very experiencing, can he but once realize it, lies the key to his problem and its solution. It is not to be found elsewhere and 'the Sexes', that is, those who are awakened to the polar tensions of their nature and who accept this despite the suffering involved, are now in a position to 'work'. This work is hard and painful, the 'swink and sweat' and the 'travail in the nought' of the uncertainty of 'Unknowing'. But it is the means of regaining Paradise, for Paradise implies integration, oneness, union with the infinite—all those things which divide us, 'the Sexes', from the 'Real Human'.

This work is the only creative process which has any real significance for man. In one of his finest designs, the colour-print entitled 'The Elohim creating Adam' (Fig. 34) at the Tate Gallery (and elsewhere), Blake has portrayed this all-important creative process with remarkable insight. The Elohim was understood by Blake to mean 'the Angel of the Divine Presence', that is, the actuality present in each moment of time.[1] Creation, in this sense, lies in time, not outside it; it is in the present, not in some remote and ideal past or future. In the picture man is shown with his lower limbs still encircled in reptilian folds; the wormlike state still partially enfolds him. Lying on the earth, above the water and beneath sun and sky, he is surrounded by the four elements. On his face is the horror and suffering of the night of experience. The Elohim, that higher potential which links him with the Divine, can only create the man, the 'Real Human', who can bear to look upon the material—all the material—out of which he has to be created.

Now returning once more to Picture 6 we can interpret it as follows. Coming at last to the stage of experience man sees that he must accept life in its entirety. He realizes that its problems cannot be solved by thought processes and will alone, nor by good intentions. He pulls aside the *veil* and looks on death, that is, the dark, difficult, suffering side of life—that inexplicable part of life which his conscious mind had so far rejected and tried to escape from. Instantly, something in him is liberated and leaps out of the chrysalis, out of the shell.

The next couplet of the text goes on to describe this situation more fully:

When weary Man enters his Cave
He meets his Saviour in the Grave.

This seemingly paradoxical experience is illustrated in a favourite composition of Blake's which he used as a frontispiece to 'Jerusalem' (Fig. 35). It shows Los entering the tomb to be with man in the 'Caverns of the Grave', and to light his way back again to life.[2]

[1] 'Thus Nature is a Vision of the Science of the Elohim.' *Milton*, plate 31, line 65 (this is the last line of the first book). Compare: 'Albion was the parent of the Druids: and in his chaotic state of sleep Satan and Adam and the Whole World was Created by the Elohim', *Jerusalem*, plate 27; preface to chap. 2, 'To the Jews'. Also *A Vision of the Last Judgment* (Keynes edition), p. 152: Jehovah Elohim 'that Angel of the Divine Presence mentioned in *Exodus*, XIV, v. 19, and in other places'.

[2] Compare the lines in *Milton*, plate 35, lines 40–41:

'For God himself enters Death's Door always with those that enter
And lays down in the Grave with them, in Visions of Eternity'.

Los is man's intuition, his power of imagination and vision. Once man can accept his weakness, his shadow-side, all that he dislikes and fears in himself, he will find a saviour, a redeeming principle at work within him. This is a fundamental idea of Blake's, which runs through all his work. The Redeemer is not only a 'God on High', but a seed hidden in the earth, in man himself.[1] Just as Urthona, which is transcendental reality beyond form and idea, lurks in essence in the deepest and darkest dens of human nature, so through the medium of Los this reality can be in contact with man and appear to him. The light which Los carries in his hand in the picture is the inner sun, the redeeming symbol which gives light and guidance even in the murky tomb of disillusion and struggle.

Death, the grave, the tomb—needless to say these refer to psychological states, not to purely physical ones. These expressions can be found in all religious mystical writings based on first-hand experience, from the New Testament down to Blake's own time. But Blake was speaking to eighteenth-century rationalist England, and to the age of positivism which was approaching. So in 'Jerusalem' he specifically says, 'O that Death and Annihilation were the same!'[2] It is still necessary to point out that the psychological, symbolic meaning of words and phrases is no less real than their concrete meaning.

The next couplet continues:

Some find a Female Garment there
And some a Male woven with care.

This refers to two aspects of the redeeming symbol, which shines from Los's lamp in the obscurity. First, there is the female garment, which is the vision of man's ideal, his pearl or treasure, as the beloved. The beloved in this symbolic sense is woman seen as man's soul-image; she holds his whole potential of love, aspiration, self-sacrifice. Dante's Beatrice is perhaps the most widely known example in art of the idealized soul-image, who leads man to his

[1] See the important stanza in *Milton*, plate 22, lines 25–40, which contains the line: 'Seek not thy heavenly father then beyond the skies'.

[2] *Jerusalem*, plate 23, line 40.

goal. As the anima, this symbol has been much studied in Jungian psychology. The anima may appear in countless different forms, but always man's relation to the anima-image is of basic importance. Blake has written a great deal about this female aspect of the redeeming symbol, and we shall return to this theme again when studying the Arlington Court picture in the next chapter. He has also drawn and painted this image from many points of view. Figure 36 is an example taken from 'Jerusalem' (plate 14) and shows Los's vision of the soul-image: 'And Los beheld the mild Emanation Jerusalem.'[1]

The male garment or symbol is the archetype which has been called by Jung the 'Puer Eternus', the Eternal Youth. The Puer Eternus is the symbol of creative possibility, the Godlike potential latent in life and waiting to be realized. It includes both the Apollonian and Dionysiac ideals of life. The Puer Eternus, like the anima, is always manifesting itself anew. Blake was very familiar with these images in his visionary experience, and he was able to indicate very subtle distinctions with regard to them. In this lies the real importance of his art, and it is without rival (so far as I know) in Western culture. For Blake, by means of the intuitive language of art, was able to convey the subtlest 'hints and indirections' about the psychology of life, which he experienced so deeply. Commentary, with its coarse thumb, can do no more than indicate certain contexts, and it only obscures the issue if it does not ultimately send the reader back to Blake himself, the enlightened man who had the rare gifts of the artist.

Among the more obvious distinctions drawn by Blake about the Puer Eternus is that concerning Orc, one of his important mythological characters. Orc represents the aggressive, energic source of man's individuality based on the instincts and physical passions. Whilst Orc has a certain relation with the Eternal Youth (for nothing in man is isolated), Orc is quite distinct from this symbol. It is a great mistake (too frequently made by Blake commentators) to confuse the spirit of aggression and self-assertion with that of the

[1] *Jerusalem*, plate 14, line 31.

ever-youthful seed of spiritual promise, even though the aggressive urge may at certain levels of development be not yet differentiated from the seed, which will one day yield the flower of liberation.

In 'America', plate 11, Blake shows the male redeeming symbol as a very young boy lying beneath the ripening corn (Fig. 37). When the corn is harvested the boy will be found living in the bread, for it is the labours of the harvest of experience which yields the bread of life.[1] It is worth comparing this image with the last two plates of 'Milton' (British Museum copy), where the theme has been developed in an extraordinarily interesting way.[2]

But it is necessary to emphasize here that the Puer Eternus and anima symbols have actually to be experienced in some form; otherwise it is useless and misleading to discuss them, or to find examples and comparisons. Without some inkling of a similar experience, which everyone may have, it cannot be a living idea. A dead symbol or image, which only lives in the intellectual function, is quite meaningless from this point of view.[3]

Blake refers to the *Male* and *Female* symbols as *Garments* because he is fully alive to the fact that a symbol is a guide to, or medium of, a particular realization. It is like a garment which is a covering of nakedness; also it is a mark of rank or occupation, like the old-fashioned tradesmen's and professional liveries, which denoted the employment of their wearers. But although it is indicative of the end in view, it is not that end or state itself; it is not its actualization and fruition. The male or female garment indicates the character of the work which has to be undertaken, the line which has to be followed.

The next couplet in the text is a warning:

Lest the Sexual Garments sweet
Should grow a devouring Winding sheet.

[1] See Blake's comments on this bread of life image, which occurs so frequently in his Prophetic Books, in *The Vision of the Last Judgment* (Keynes edition), vol. iii, p. 156.

[2] Plates 44, 45 (British Museum copy).

[3] W. B. Yeats's 'Song of Wandering Aengus' is a beautiful example of the anima symbol, based on a Celtic legend. A remarkable use of this symbol is contained in poem xviii of *The Song of Life*, by J. Krishnamurti ('Ah, the symphony of that song!').

The redeeming symbols are like a beacon light, they give a sense of direction and show the way. Without them man is at a loss, he is 'mere passion and appetite', as Blake says.[1] Without them he will sink deeper into confusion, disillusion, deeper into maya.[2] This downward moving path of confusion and attachment is illustrated in the Arlington Court picture, in the bottom left section (Fig. 55). This is the state of the *devouring Winding sheet*.

PICTURE 7 (Fig. 9). Inscribed: *Alas, what are these?* This picture and the following are concerned with what may be loosely called the difficulties of the way. The couplet referring to this picture, which at first presents something of a puzzle, reads:

One Dies! Alas! the Living & Dead
One is slain & One is fled.

This refers to the illusion of time and the human tendency to be so preoccupied with the past and future that man fails to give himself completely to the living moment in the present. But life, reality, only exists in the present. Blake wrote two well-known epigrams on this theme. One of them is:

He who bends to himself a joy
Doth the winged life destroy;
But he who kisses the joy as it flies
Lives in eternity's sunrise.[3]

Here in the picture, the joy, the fullness, and opportunity of the moment, is seen in flight. Another, which has been grasped with the intention of retaining it and clinging to it, lies dead. For it is just in this that we are so often at fault in our actual experience. This is the art of life to which so few have found the secret. Either we miss what the moment offers, and it flies away for ever; or, by trying to bend it to our will and purpose, we destroy it.

[1] *Milton*, plate 28, lines 23–30.
[2] Compare the description of this in *Milton*, plate 48.
[3] Keynes edition, vol. i, p. 241. 'Bends' is now sometimes read as 'binds'. It is obscure in the Rossetti Note-Book, p. 105 (reversed).

But Blake is also pointing to a deeper problem connected with this. Under the picture, as well as the brief inscription, is written:

What are these? Alas! the Female Martyr
Is She also the Divine Image?

The idea at which he is hinting is that in each moment of life there is a death of one thing that another may live; a sacrifice of one value that another may come into being. More specifically, there is an allusion to the sacrifice which the female, receptive, conditioned aspect of life has to make in order to find itself at one with the creative, formative principle. The *Divine Image* springs from the reconciliation of the two opposites, or contrary states (as Blake termed them); for these two contraries are always present and without them there is no life. In 'Milton' Blake devoted a whole plate of the text to the elucidation of this principle.[1] The 'happy female joy', as he there terms it, is only actualized in self-sacrifice, just as the male principle can only realize itself in redeeming the female, again by apparent self-annihilation. This law of life appears as self-sacrifice and self-abandonment, but really it is the way to creative life. Yet instead of this, the one aspect, or life-principle, is always trying to impose itself on the other, which leads only to destruction, sterility.

This is undoubtedly the inner meaning of the so-called 'Good and Evil Angels' (Fig. 38), the well-known colour-print reproduced here from the example in the Tate Gallery. An early version of this design is found in 'The Marriage of Heaven and Hell'.[2] There, it illustrates the struggle between the two contrary states, the two seemingly opposite aspects of life: passion, emotion, desire, on the one hand, and the ideal of reason and order on the other. Life, the 'Infant Joy',[3] shown as the child in the picture, lies eternally between the two, though it is always being snatched away by the one or the other (in this design, the principle of reason and order). Each time

[1] Plate 36. Compare the poem 'My Spectre around me' (Keynes edition, vol. ii, p. 210).
[2] Plate 4 (Fitzwilliam Museum copy).
[3] See *Jerusalem*, plate 22, lines 19–24.

this happens there is disaster, as Blake clearly demonstrates in the illustration which follows in 'The Marriage'.[1]

Neither side, or principle, can be called good or evil; these terms, like heaven and hell, are entirely relative, as Blake never tires of insisting. Life springs eternally into being between the play of the opposites; the opposites or contraries are both real and must eternally endure. But life, reality, lies in neither contrary. It is the ever-living youthful third which springs from them.

In the next picture, and the four which follow, Blake continues pointing to particular difficulties which beset the way of experience, and make its tortuous paths and by-ways so difficult to unravel.

PICTURE 8. Inscribed: *My Son! My Son!* (Fig. 10). This is the problem of authority, of domination, and of the conforming to an ideal, which is based on habit and not understanding. It refers not only to external authority, but also to the tyranny which is set up within, in the mind and will. This psychological tyranny, the arbitrary dominion of one part of our psychosomatic make-up over the rest, is called by Blake the 'Spectre'. The Spectre is the false tyrant set up by, and identified with, the ego.

Two couplets comment on this picture:

In Vain-glory hatcht & nurst
By double Spectres Self Accurst
My Son! My Son! thou treatest me
But as I have instructed thee.

Reproduced in Figure 39 is an illustration of the Spectre from 'Jerusalem'.[2] Blake identifies the Spectre with the 'Selfhood', or ego-personality, and with the rational, thinking function. The *vain-glory* mentioned in the couplet refers to the extraordinary over-valuation of the ego which afflicts all people brought up in our Western culture. When the Spectre or ego-personality becomes inflated and begins to usurp a position which does not rightfully belong to it—when a tyranny of the part is in this way set up over the whole—then we are cursed by the Spectre and manacled with his chain. Blake has described and commented on this at length in

[1] Which shows the fall of a horse and rider.

[2] Plate 6.

passages in 'Milton' and 'Jerusalem', and particularly in his short poem 'My Spectre around me Night and Day'.[1]

But he speaks here of a double Spectre: *By double Spectres Self Accurst.* This other aspect of the Spectre is less personal; it is a more unconscious attachment to authority, such as is described by Freud as the Super-ego, by Jung as the Father-figure; it is also manifested in the perennial over-evaluation of the Master or Guru, named by Jung the archetype of the Wise Old Man. In this sense, Blake is referring to a rigid, authoritarian moral law which is passed on to the son from the father, or from the cultural tradition. It is the abuse, the inflation of this law which constitutes the evil. Blake was very much alive to the dangers of this, and realized that conventional manners hid evils which had a firm hold at unconscious levels:

> A man's worst enemies are those
> Of his own house and family;
> And he who makes his law a curse
> By his own law shall surely die.[2]

So, in Picture 8 of the series, the arrow is pointed at the Father, who stands not only for the personal father, but also the social and cultural tradition. Repression in one sphere is bound to cause a vicious eruption in another.

The result of the growth and inflation of the Spectre is a repression of the unconscious. The irrational instinctive and feeling side of life gets cut off from the rational, conscious side. But we depend as much on the one as the other. Dire consequences inevitably follow on this inharmonious, diseased state of affairs.

In 'Jerusalem' Blake illustrates this unfortunate psychological situation, which he expands there in the text at great length (Fig. 40).[3] Above is Albion—the Everyman who has fallen into this state; he is sinking down in a condition of collapse. Los, his imaginative, intuitive faculty, is trying to rescue him and is bending over him.

[1] Keynes edition, vol. ii, p. 210. A key passage in *Milton* is: plate 15, lines 14–32; also plate 41, lines 44–46. Also, *Jerusalem*, plates 6–10, &c.

[2] *Jerusalem*, plate 27, prologue to chap. 2, lines 98–101.

[3] Stirling copy, plate 37 (Keynes edition, plate 37; monochrome facsimile of Rinder copy, plate 33).

But Albion's Spectre is brooding like a great vulture, or bat, over his female, unconscious part. There, in the female, in the depths of the unconscious, lies his soul-energy; that is the place where (in a psychological figure of speech) the sun and moon shine. But all this is cut off from above by the brooding vulture, and the female, his anima, is shown lying pale, cold, rigid in death.

The curse of the Spectre is shown from another point of view in one of Blake's most terrifying designs (Fig. 41). This comes from the Job series and shows Job's oppressive dreams.[1] Here Blake shows the results of a dangerous inflation of the self-righteous man, who clings rigidly by conscious effort to the moral law. The unconscious, which should be man's friend, but whose voice has been habitually rejected, becomes full of threatening and fearful forms—these are shown reaching up at Job from beneath his bed. The conscious side, which contains the God of his morality, begins to transform into the Devil itself. The Godlike figure who oppresses Job from above already has the cloven hoof of the devil. This is the basic problem of the rationalistic man who is striving after an ideal. For Blake he is typified in the person of Job, and his twenty-one engraved plates entitled 'Illustrations of the Book of Job' are a commentary on this theme, which Blake seems rightly to have regarded as of cardinal importance for Western man, who is culturally conditioned by Judaic-Christian (in England predominantly Protestant) thought. An extremely interesting parallel to Blake's work on this theme is provided in a remarkable book written by James Hogg (the self-taught shepherd of Ettrick) in about 1824 (that is, contemporary with Blake's last years). 'The Private Memoirs and Confessions of a Justified Sinner' is a phantasy loaded with psychological meaning;[2] it describes the same type of self-righteous personality set against a Calvinist background and it is an altogether original and sinister story.

[1] *Illustrations of the Book of Job,* plate 11. There is a remarkable coloured version of this design in the Fitzwilliam Museum, reproduced here.

[2] James Hogg, *The Private Memoirs and Confessions of a Justified Sinner* (The Cresset Press, 1947); first published 1824. Miss Barbara Hannah, of the C. G. Jung Institute, Zürich, has lectured on this book.

PICTURE 9. Climbing to the Moon (Fig. 11). Inscription: *I want! I want!* The couplet reads:

On the shadows of the Moon
Climbing thro Nights highest noon.

But there is no solution either in the endless pursuit of desire. Man always wants more, the bigger and the better; to seek the gratification of desire is to 'cry for the moon'. Desire can only be overcome by a bigger, stronger desire. But there may be another approach to the problem of desire, which is neither that of repression, nor the endless pursuit of gratification.

It seems that Blake has attempted to express the possibility and the nature of the solution to this problem in one of his water-colours from the Paradise Regained series, which illustrates 'Jesus refusing the Banquet' (Fig. 43).[1] The Tempter proffers the banquet to Jesus and he is offered gratification of the senses and physical appetites in full measure. But somehow Jesus does not seem to see them in this way and for him there is clearly no temptation. That is, there is no division between tempting offer, desire, and refusal.

PICTURE 10. Time's Ocean (Fig. 12). Inscribed: *Help! Help!* The line from the text is: *In Times Ocean falling drownd.* The ocean here is the sea of time, man's karma; it is the conditioned past which overwhelms man with its weight of habit. It is the accumulation of worldly experience and mechanical reaction which gradually submerges life. This picture follows on that about desire because it is failure to discriminate that leads to this kind of psychological submersion and drowning. Lack of discrimination is due to the underdevelopment of the feeling function, the emotional side of life in all its many aspects. For, as well as intellectual discrimination, there is also the discrimination of feeling, and it is just this which was, and is, habitually neglected in deference to the cultivation of intellect, both in Blake's day and in our own. The awareness which comes from the development and discrimination of feeling is absolutely necessary

[1] Fitzwilliam Museum, *c.* 1808.

for the mature human being. The picture is a comment on the fate of those who neglect it.

In his water colour, 'David delivered out of many waters' (Fig. 42),[1] Blake shows David on the point of drowning in this ocean of enmeshing circumstance and karma. But the poet in David, his development of his intuitive and feeling sides, leads to his deliverance.

Time's ocean, as referred to here, must be distinguished from the sea of the unconscious with its life-giving energies, which is another image with quite different emphasis that is frequently found in Blake's work. We shall meet it in the next chapter in connexion with the Arlington Court picture.

PICTURE 11. *Aged Ignorance* is the title given to this illustration (Fig. 13). This refers to the tendency to try to explain everything in life by the known; to reduce everything to fit in with a preconceived formula. But if everything inexplicable is rejected, and if anything adventurous, disturbing, and challenging is refused, then life itself dries up. For life is the unknown, and the over-valuation of rational and moral perfection results, not in superior achievement, but rather in a measure of unrelatedness and stagnation. Blake had already expressed himself passionately on this theme in 'The Marriage of Heaven and Hell'. Here he comments in the inscription:

Perceptive Organs closed, their Objects close

which echoes the inscription under the frontispiece, with which we began:

The Sun's Light when he unfolds it
Depends on the Organ that beholds it.

The couplet in the text comments on this picture:

In Aged Ignorance profound
Holy & cold I clipd the Wings
Of all Sublunary Things.

This picture indicates the path which leads towards the Limit of Opaqueness. Opaqueness, as already explained (pp. 10–11), is Blake's term for lack of imagination, sympathy, insight, and vision.

[1] In the Tate Gallery; usually associated with *Psalm* XVIII, v. 16.

Opaqueness stands at the opposite end of the pole from lucidity. The limits of opaqueness and contraction are two very important ideas for Blake; beyond these two limits a man loses his human quality. We have now caught a glimpse of the road which leads to the limit of opaqueness.[1]

What Blake here refers to as Ignorance is paradoxically the attempt to explain everything; it is the attempt to set up one part of man's nature as the absolute measure of the whole. Endeavouring to become a superman by an act of will, we distort our true manhood. This is the danger referred to in the mysterious line in 'The Four Zoas'; 'In attempting to become more than man we become less'.[2] In the present context Blake is pointing to this danger particularly in connexion with the thinking or intellectual function, which in Blake's age, as in our own, is the most developed and highly valued of man's psychic functions. For this reason Newton stood for Blake as the exemplar of opaqueness.[3]

Blake regarded Sir Isaac Newton, the mathematician and astronomer, as the instigator of eighteenth-century rationalism and deism. Blake saw in these the worst manifestations of rational mind functioning in its most limited ways. Eighteenth-century rationalism excluded everything which it could not measure, and deism attempted to explain everything in relation to logical thought processes. It was the danger inherent in the abuse of these one-sided attitudes against which Blake protested.

The well-known colour-print of 'Newton' (Fig. 45), reproduced here from the Tate Gallery example, is a satire on the limitations of one-pointed concentration, intellectual knowledge, and exclusive reliance on rational measure. Newton's contracted posture in this picture is reminiscent of the figure representing Air, number four of our series (Fig. 6). Thought is both the grandest and the most limiting of man's functions, and if over-developed without due relationship being maintained with other functions, it leads to the most materialistic forms of servitude.

[1] Compare *Milton*, plate 31, lines 35–39.

[2] *The Four Zoas*, book 9, line 709.

[3] For references on the *Limits of Opaqueness and Contraction* (or *Solidity*), see p. 10, n. 2.

None the less, it is only when the limit of opaqueness has been seen, that is, when the fault has been fully manifested and so apprehended and realized, that it is possible to be free from it. This is one of Blake's central ideas, as he explains in his notes on 'A Vision of the Last Judgment': error must be clearly seen to be cast out. Only with such a realization can a 'Last Judgment', or moment of enlightenment, come about.[1]

This principle is illustrated in plate 13 of 'Europe' (Fig. 44).[2] The man in chains is Orc; Orc represents the aggressive, revolutionary instinct in man. In the Prophetic Book, 'Europe', Orc has tried to free mankind from the rationalistic and political despotism which has been stifling eighteenth-century Europe. Orc has tried to seize the trumpet of the Last Judgment and to blow it. But he cannot. Then Newton takes the trumpet and blows it; a Last Judgment is sounded. The meaning is that when a man clearly sees what limits and enthrals him, then there is the possibility of liberation. Once the nature of opaqueness is realized, and its myopic quality is perceived, then one begins to look for the light. Newton is shown in the picture beginning to ascend the stairs with the keys of his prison doors in his hand.

So much for the idea of opaqueness. In the next picture we are shown the limit of contraction.

PICTURE 12. Ugolino (Fig. 14). This design was used in the 'Marriage of Heaven and Hell' and is associated with the story in Dante's 'Inferno' about Count Ugolino and the traitorous bishop. In the course of political intrigue Ugolino was betrayed and imprisoned with his children in a dungeon; the keys of the prison were then thrown into the river and the father and children were left to die. The story was popular in the late eighteenth century, and the design was a favourite of Blake's to which he returned more than once.[3] The couplet reads:

And in depths of my Dungeons
Closed the Father & the Sons.

[1] Keynes edition, vol. iii, pp. 145–62.

[2] British Museum copy.

[3] *Marriage of Heaven and Hell*, plate 16 (Fitzwilliam Museum copy). Later in the 'Hunger

This fate, the limit of contraction, is the psychological equivalent of the failure to develop one's talents. Caught in the toils of the world, man fails to develop or allow the expression of the divine spark within. Thus he becomes the 'worm seventy inches long'. Under this illustration is written: *Does thy God, O Priest, take such Vengeance as this?* Blake is here stressing the fact that it is within a man's own choice whether he reduces himself to such a state, and allows himself to become identified with one or other of these limits. This is the choice which Blake indicated in the frontispiece. The other alternative, the state of 'Glad Day', is also open to him. But it is easy to be betrayed by the false gods of ambition or security, who are always striving to set up their idols within us.

One of the most frightening of Blake's pictures is the 'House of Death' (or Lazar House), here illustrated from the colour-print in the Tate Gallery (Fig. 46). This is a picture of psychological death, the torture and decay which results from being cut off from the light and source of life. The picture, as the title suggests, is perhaps connected with the passage in Milton's 'Paradise Lost', Book XI,[1] which describes Adam's first horrifying vision of death, to which before his fall he had been a total stranger.

Who is the god presiding over this dungeon of death, this scene of apparent vengeance and tyranny? It is man's own mind, the false tyrant within. Very significant is the degenerate, murderous figure with the dagger on the right. This is the traitor, the enemy within, the renegade.[2] The powers of life have turned against themselves and become the powers of death. This is the psychological meaning of the picture, which as in all Blake's art is paramount. But it remains meaningless and valueless unless the image itself can be reached subjectively. Then it will reveal itself as an experience with significance beyond the reach of words. A vision of such consequence

Tower', second illustration to the story among the Dante designs. See Frances A. Yates's article on 'Ugolino' in the *Journal of the Warburg Institute*, vol. xiv (1951), pp. 92–117 (113–14 on Blake).

[1] *Paradise Lost*, Book XI, lines 477–96.

[2] See *Europe*, Preludium, plate 4 (Fitzwilliam Museum, Riches copy), for another aspect of this renegade figure. But in the *Europe* design, it is the more positive figure of the aggressive Orc, who is shown threatening the traveller (clad in blue), who stands for the persona.

as this is not a pleasant thing. But it is salutary and beneficial in proportion to the force of its terror and horror.

PICTURE 13. Vision (Fig. 15). Inscribed: *Fear and Hope are—Vision*. After these two limits of opaqueness and contraction have been recognized, then comes the understanding of the meaning of vision. There is a sudden glimpse of the relativity of everything, especially mental values with their opposites, such as hope and fear. With this may come the realization of the essential nature of intuitive imagination. The art of life is based on this faculty, which is one with creative affirmation or faith, and there is no escape from it in the direction of some apparently more certain and measurable standard of values.

Vision, or imagination, gives insight into the positive and negative aspects of life, but above all into their absolute relativity. It sees the limits of things and therefore it is the great unifier. Blake gives a striking example of this in the fourth 'Memorable Fancy' in 'The Marriage of Heaven and Hell'. He there describes his vision of the black and white spiders and of the monstrous serpent. But Blake was determined to see this horrific aspect of life to its end; he persisted, and suddenly the scene turned into one of the utmost tranquillity and beauty.[1] So also, in the 'Illustrations of the Book of Job', he faced up to the horrific aspect of nature, which he there termed Behemoth and Leviathan. The engraved plate, which is reproduced here (Fig. 48), is of the utmost interest with regard to the problem of evil and fear.[2] He inscribed this engraving with the text:

> Behemoth is the chief of the ways of God
> Leviathan is King over the children of Pride
> Behold now Behemoth which I made with thee.

There is also the transcendental experience of the unitive power of the intuitive imagination, the 'Divine Vision and Fruition, in which Man liveth Eternally'.[3] In 'Milton' Blake described and illustrated

[1] *Marriage of Heaven and Hell*; the fourth Memorable Fancy (Keynes edition, vol. i, pp. 190–2).

[2] *Illustrations of the Book of Job*, plate 15.

[3] *Milton*, plate 35, lines 8–29. Among Blake's many statements on this theme, see *Jerusalem*, plate 77: 'To the Christians' (Prologue to chap. 4): 'I know of no other Christianity and of no other Gospel than the liberty both of body and mind to exercise the Divine Arts of Imagination, the real and eternal World of which this Vegetable Universe is but a faint shadow. . . '.

such a transcendental experience (Fig. 47). He tells how Los entered into him and he became one with Los:

> Los descended to me:
> And Los behind me stood, a terrible flaming Sun, just close
> Behind my back . . .
> And I became One Man with him arising in my strength.[1]

PICTURE 14. (Fig. 16). Inscribed: *The Traveller hasteth in the Evening*. The couplet referring to *Vision* joins with the following about this picture of the traveller:

> *But when once I did descry*
> *The Immortal Man that cannot Die*
> *Thro evening shades I haste away*
> *To close the Labours of my Day.*

When a glimpse of the true nature of life has been perceived, then the *Traveller* makes haste to return from the Night Journey, from the 'travail in the murkness'. The *Traveller hasteth* because, now he has had a realization of the *Immortal Man*, his orientation has completely changed. He hastens to conclude the labours of his day; that is, the concerns which were formerly so important for him and formed the main preoccupation of his life, now appear to him as delusions to which he has been quite wrongly subservient. He has a new sense of direction and a new sense of his rightful task as a man.

But he must first conclude his labours, although what appeared to him once as daylight now appears more like the shades of evening. He must complete the task of coming to terms with his experience, which began with his hatching from the egg in the sixth picture of the series. Until he has fully explored his own 'eternal lineaments' he cannot obtain release. Only when he has solved the enmeshing illusions of his own nature can he return, as the traveller now wishes to do. This is emphasized in the next picture with its accompanying text.

PICTURE 15. *Death's Door* (Fig. 17). For this picture seems to

[1] *Milton*, plate 24. British Museum copy, plate 27.

show us the very opposite to the expected release and return. Instead of a triumphal apotheosis or ascent into heaven, Blake shows us a picture labelled *Death's Door*. The couplet reads:

> *The Door of Death I open found*
> *And the Worm Weaving in the Ground.*

Surely the meaning of this is to emphasize the fact again that true vision implies accepting the dark side of life so completely that the *door* to it remains permanently open. In this sense vision, or intuitive imagination, really is liberation; there is no more need to separate the light from the dark, the temptation from the resistance, life from death. If heaven, earth, and hell are to live in harmony, as Blake insists they must, then the earth and hell must be as fully accepted as heaven:

> Therefore I print: nor vain my types shall be:
> Heaven, Earth and Hell, henceforth shall live in harmony.[1]

As long as the opposites exist independently and in conflict with one another, they have no meaning. They are given meaning and harmony only in that reality which exists beyond them and includes them in itself.

In 'Milton', Blake has given illuminating expression to this theme. The Puritan poet Milton had tried to escape to heaven leaving a large part of his life unresolved. Blake, in his poem, brings him back to earth again to redeem and reintegrate his unresolved problems, exemplified in his three quarrelsome wives and daughters. Plate 13 of 'Milton' shows him preparing to descend (Fig. 49).[2] He discards the 'Robe of Promise' and the 'Girdle of the Oath of God', which are two symbols for the positive, Apollonian side of his nature. For he goes to meet his rejected shadow-side, all the warring forces within him which he could not previously accept, understand, and so redeem. The robe and the girdle must be temporarily discarded by the man who undertakes the Night Journey.

[1] *Jerusalem*, plate 3, Prologue 'To the Public'.
[2] British Museum copy, plate 13; Keynes edition, plate 15.

Milton descends and Blake receives him like a falling star in his left foot. The accompanying picture illustrates this mythical scene (Fig. 50).[1] Blake knew the worth of his own lowest aspect, all that is most rejected and despised, typified by the left foot; the divine spark is present there as much as anywhere. In the dust of his own experience, even in the meanest of it and the soiled, he knew his eternal star was to be found:[2]

> And all this Vegetable World appear'd on my left Foot
> As a bright sandal form'd immortal of precious stones and gold.
> I stooped down and bound it on to walk forward thro' Eternity.[3]

PICTURE 16. The Worm-Mother (Fig. 18). This is the final picture in the series, except for the illustration inset in the epilogue. It is inscribed:

> *I have said to the Worm*
> *Thou art my mother and my sister.*

Here sits the female goddess of Nature, the female which rose from man's *Darkness* when he lost touch with the 'Eternal Great Humanity', as described in the first couplet. Unregenerate man is ruled by this goddess. Aspiring man struggles with her. Regenerate man regards her as a mother and a sister, because he is free of her dominion. The two couplets read:

> *Thou'rt my Mother from the Womb*
> *Wife Sister Daughter to the Tomb*
> *Weaving to Dreams the Sexual strife*
> *And weeping over the Web of Life.*

The realm of the female goddess, the dark, conditioned, Yin side of life, is by itself a place of weeping, of strife, of illusion. It has to be redeemed by its opposite, the contrary state, the light, formative, Apollonian, or Yang side. The ignorant man wanders away into the

[1] British Museum copy, plate 29.

[2] Compare the saying of Morienus: 'Take that which is trodden underfoot upon the dung-heap; if you do not, when you wish to climb the stairs, you will fall down upon your head.' (Quoted by Jung, *Integration of the Personality*, p. 268.) See also Krishnamurti's poem in *The Song of Life*, no. xxvii, 'O Friend thou canst not bind Truth'.

[3] *Milton*, plate 23, lines 4–14 (Keynes edition).

realm of the Mother, and the farther he goes the more hopeless his lot becomes.

This was the fate of Achan, as Blake understood the Biblical story in Joshua, chapter 7. Achan identified himself with his shadow-side, became a criminal, stole the treasure consecrated to Jehovah. The moral law condemned Achan to death by stoning, as a punishment. Figure 51 shows Blake's illustration of this story.[1]

But, says Blake, this attitude of condemnation and punishment is utterly wrong. Instead of curing the evil it only creates fresh evil. The understanding which comes through acceptance, and which implies forgiveness, is what is needed:

Mutual Forgiveness of each Vice
Such are the Gates of Paradise.

In plate 25 of 'Jerusalem' he illustrates the possibility of this attitude in a picture of extraordinary psychological interest (Fig. 52). It is worth noticing that the posture of the man in this picture is similar to Achan's.

The context in 'Jerusalem' describes how man has fallen under the sway of nature, the dark goddess. He has become racked with conflict and contorted in agony, just as Achan was at his stoning. In the illustration, the signs of his psycho-somatic functions are all misplaced on his body and limbs, showing his degree of disorientation. But the 'Daughters of Beulah' weep over him. The 'Daughters of Beulah' are man's own inherent powers of recovering his inner harmony and sense of direction.[2] They hold him by secret threads and a sort of psychological umbilical cord. They represent the power of the imagination to throw up symbols and present them intuitively to the mind (as these symbols come from the region of the mind most remote and other from ego-consciousness, they appear to come from the unconscious). By means of these symbols, which are the 'Daughters of Beulah', the lost man can be rescued.

[1] Water-colour, 'The Stoning of Achan'. In the Tate Gallery. Inscribed on back: 'The Blasphemer. And Moses spake unto the Children of Israel.' Lev. xxiv. 23.

[2] A key passage on Beulah, one of Blake's most frequently used symbols, is plate 33 of *Milton*. See also *Milton*, plate 38, lines 8–18.

Although they may become more and more obscure and tenuous the farther he sinks into the meshes of maya, yet the threads are always there and they do not break. The compassion of the 'Daughters of Beulah' endures, as does man's capacity for acceptance and assimilation.

EPILOGUE

The Epilogue is addressed to the Accuser, Satan:

To The Accuser who is
The God of This World.

The Epilogue reads (first stanza):

Truly My Satan thou art but a Dunce
And dost not know the Garment from the Man
Every Harlot was a Virgin once
Nor canst thou ever change Kate into Nan.

The individual, says Blake, is not the same as the state in which he is. Man passes through states, in the course of experience, as he puts on or changes his clothes.[1] *The Accuser* who holds him responsible to a moral law is the God of society, of *This World.* This may be necessary for society and these laws may be in order from the point of view of social organization, but from the point of view of the individual this affords no help and it offers him no solution. The individual has to realize that the forces of life, whether they manifest as good or evil, eternally endure. His realization must transcend *This World* with its moral codes and ideals.

The Epilogue concludes (second stanza):

Tho' thou art Worship'd by the Names Divine
Of Jesus & Jehovah: thou art still
The Son of Morn in weary Night's decline
The lost Traveller's Dream under the Hill.

[1] See *A Vision of the Last Judgment* (Keynes edition), vol. iii, p. 148 (which is p. 80 of the Rossetti MS.); also p. 149 (Rossetti MS., pp. 76–77). Compare *Milton,* plate 35.

Man's idea of God, which he raises on his *altars high*, is only a projection of himself. It is only a projection of an arbitrary, isolated part of his total being, which in reality and in its totality is one with the 'Divine Humanity'.[1] This projected image, call it by what name you will, is ultimately man's greatest enemy. It is a mental phenomenon, which springs from the mind and is limited by the mind. It is the *dream* of the *traveller* who has gone astray, who has lost his way. It is necessary to realize the illusion of this.

The illustration which concludes this pictorial treatise (Fig. 19), shows this projected image which man calls God, not recognizing it as part of himself. It is shown as a devil with batlike wings rising out of the sleeping traveller. It is man's Spectre.

Blake was aware that reality, or God, is beyond idea and form. The projection, the Spectre, has to be realized and so overthrown, as we saw in Figure 25 (see page 18). This is the cardinal idea in all Blake's writing and in all his art. This idea Blake has expressed in one simple image. It is the picture he used as a frontispiece to 'Europe' in 1794 (which is sometimes called 'Urizen-creator'). He repeated it several times and it was the last picture he worked at and completed on his death-bed in 1827 (Fig. 53).[2] This is not a picture of God creating the Universe, as is sometimes naïvely assumed. It might almost be said to be exactly the reverse, for 'Error is created. Truth is Eternal.'[3] This is the image of the mind creating, or projecting, its own Maya. Blake has stated this in the plainest terms in an epigram, entitled 'To God':

> If you have formed a Circle to go into
> Go into yourself, and see how you would do.[4]

The person who can attain an insight into this image for himself will know the source of his greatest illusion and bondage.

[1] See *Milton*, plate 23, lines 58–60 to plate 24, lines 1–3. Also *A Vision of the Last Judgment* (Keynes edition, vol. iii, p. 156): 'All Springing from the Divine Humanity. All beams from him.'

[2] The version illustrated is taken from the British Museum copy of *Europe*. The 1827 version, the last he did, is at The Whitworth Art Gallery, Manchester.

[3] *A Vision of the Last Judgment* (Keynes edition, vol. iii, p. 162). 'Error is Created. Truth is Eternal. Error or Creation, will be Burned up, and then, and not till then, Truth or Eternity will appear. It is Burnt up the Moment Men cease to behold it.'

[4] Keynes edition, vol. iii, p. 83.

II

THE ARLINGTON COURT PICTURE: REGENERATION

William Blake believed that the expression of human experience in art and poetry was an important function of living. Everyone dreams, cogitates, asks questions of life. Most people could, if they wanted, use art in one of its many forms—painting, sculpture, poetry, music, acting—as part of the serious, but pleasurable, study and business of life. Art is as important a part of living as is any other serious activity. In a letter written to the *Monthly Magazine* about the year 1806/7, Blake in defending his friend the painter Fuseli, burst out with the affirmation of this idea:

But Oh, Englishmen! Know that every man ought to be a judge of pictures, and every man is so who has not been connoisseured out of his senses.[1]

Blake meant his art to be understood, experienced, explored. His drawing and painting, like his poetic writing, is always primarily devoted to the psychological meaning of experience. To anyone who is at all aware of subjective states and who has made any attempt to study his own dreams and phantasies, this is at once apparent. Nor are Blake's images and symbols, by means of which he expresses himself, so very strange and unfamiliar. But of course it is necessary to become acquainted with the cast of Blake's mind, as shown in a fair amount of his work. Even one's own dreams have to be studied in their proper context and over a considerable period, if one really wishes to understand them. The same obviously applies to Blake's imaginative art. Moreover, Blake has very exceptional things to say; the thoughts and feelings he has to impart are often

1 *The Letters of William Blake.* Edited by A. G. B. Russell (Methuen, 1906), Letter 50.

very subtle. His means of expression, it is true, is quite unusually intuitional, which makes it difficult for people trained almost entirely in intellectual thought processes; but the inspiration of his art is on that account all the more valuable in our age. Besides, the quality and breadth of his realization is something utterly unique, which well repays some study.

It was only in comparatively recent times, during the two centuries before Blake's birth in the middle eighteenth-century, that the study of the inner world of subjective experience became an unusual and unfamiliar subject of interest. In the Middle Ages introverted research and study was regarded not only as something quite normal and respectable, but even as an essential human task. In fact, it was then held that it was the most important business that a man could be about, if he was capable of it. Contemplation, the part of Mary, was regarded as the better part of life. It was just the same in the great civilizations of the East. The quality and importance of Blake's work would have been immediately realized in lands where the Upanishads were familiar, and where such texts as the Diamond Sutra, the Lankavatara Sutra, or the Mathnawi of Jalalu'ddin Rumi were seriously and widely studied. Indeed, there have been long epochs of time, and widely dispersed communities, in which Blake might have lived with the certainty of being regarded as a sage of the highest order. But William Blake lived in rationalistic, materialistic, mercantile England of the eighteenth century: he was almost totally ignored, and it was even surreptitiously put about that he was mentally deranged. It is now, at last, no longer necessary to make excuses for him, or to try to prove that the particular direction his art took was not due to some form of insanity. Thanks to the entirely new attitude to psychology which has developed in the present century, it is possible to approach Blake without any particular feeling of eccentricity.

The Arlington Court picture is an extremely important work of art devoted to a central human theme, namely that of regeneration. It is important to approach this picture simply and directly, as it is the result of a deep inner experience, which can again be realized through this medium. It contains an image, which may suddenly flower again into life. It may help another individual to a moment of insight. It is therefore worth treating this picture as all great works of art should be treated, that is, as precious objects of rare value, whose meaning may be won by care and devotion, but cannot be extorted.

The elucidation and commentary which follows, therefore, begins with a general description, clarified by reference to the detailed sections of the picture given in the reproductions (Figs. 54–59). Next there follows an interpretation in general terms, yielding an approximate meaning such as anyone with a little insight and psychological experience, but without any special familiarity with Blake, might find in it. Then, after this, I will proceed to relate the details of the picture to the wider terms of reference which are available in Blake's copious work, expressed in his paintings, engravings, and his poetical and Prophetic writings. In this extended context, the theme of the picture will begin to appear a very familiar one, in its broad outlines, to those who have studied Blake. Yet I will endeavour to amplify the images and symbols of the picture in a suggestive way, rather than in an analytical and explicit manner. For the meaning of the picture is held implicitly in its image and must be approached imaginatively.

BRIEF DESCRIPTION OF THE PICTURE

The man kneeling or crouching on the sea-shore, with his hands outstretched to the wild ocean, first commands the attention (Figs. 54 and 56). He wears a robe of deep red, or crimson, and is looking earnestly at the spectator. Immediately on his left, in the centre of the picture, stands a radiant female with a transparent veil and garment of iridescent hue covering her body (Fig. 57). With her right hand she points down to the man beside her, with her left upwards to where above, in the sky, four horses are being groomed by female attendants (Fig. 58). The horses are harnessed to a chariot in which a nimbed and auraed man with a sceptre is reclining, apparently asleep (Fig. 56). More female figures, some with musical instruments, are gathered round the chariot. Immediately below this chariot in the heavens, another chariot is moving over the sea, with four dark horses driven by a naked woman with windswept hair (Fig. 56). In the sea, beside the horses, two small human figures (a man and woman) are meeting the chariot as it approaches.

In the right half of the picture the land rises above the sea in cliffs (Fig. 59). A hill dominates this part of the picture and it is important to notice that this hill appears to be on fire: flames are playing over the hillside and are issuing in red and angry tongues of fire from the bottom of the steps and the roots of the trees. (The flames are quite clear in the original picture, because of their colour, but in a black and white reproduction they need pointing out.) On this hillside are groups of spinners and weavers, some with thread or yarn, others plying the shuttle, which is raised high in the right hand. Two others (on the right) hold a rope attached to a net. On the lower steps a woman, carrying a bucket, is prominent. High above, in a sort of grove or arbour, is seen a procession of winged angelic figures who are carrying tall vessels on their heads. At the bottom of this hill, in the foreground of the picture below the steps, there flows a river whose dark waters terminate on the left near the sea. A barrel or tub (at bottom right) indicates, according to the painter's convention, that a river is here intended. Reclining over this barrel or culvert is a girl or nixie, half submerged in the water. The group of writhing figures on the left (Fig. 55) also have a tub or barrel beneath them, from which the waters issue. This tormented group of writhing, nude forms is composed of three females and one male, who is horned and holds a hank of rope in his right hand. This rope passes over the others, who all hold it, or touch it, and one on the extreme left is cutting the rope where the waters of the river and sea appear to converge.

The right side of the picture is framed between two pairs of trees (Figs. 54, 59). The further landscape rises in terraces above the sea; there is a classical temple beside the shore in the distance. Higher up, three river-gods or goddesses (shown as a pair, male and female, below the arbour) recline on the slopes pouring their streams.

GENERAL INTERPRETATION

Now what do the images of this picture imply? The dramatic moment which is enacted here is centred in the man in the red robe, who is kneeling or crouching on the ocean's brink with outstretched arms. His gesture is one of calming the stormy sea, of inducting its wild power. In this moment of crisis he is linked with the radiant woman by his side, and the drama includes the charioteer above, and the chariot driving over the waves below.

The wild, dark, storm-tossed sea, which strikes such a dominant note in the picture, expresses the power of nature; not only nature which is external to man and of which he is a part, but also his own instinctive and unconscious nature within. The wild ocean represents all that stands outside conscious control, the dynamic forces of life beyond the known confines of the personality, in all their unbounded energy and vastness. This is how the unconscious is habitually seen in dreams and visions, particularly when it is a question of contrast and opposition between the consciousness of the ego-personality and the unconscious.[1] In this sort of context, the sea of the primordial unconscious always contains, as here, a double aspect of power and energy on the one hand, and of something threatening and fearful on the other.

The woman, or goddess, who rides over the sea in her chariot is a personification of the primordial forces of nature, whose domain is the unconscious with its instinctive urges and drives. Her hair is arranged above her forehead like the crescent lunar horns of Artemis, the mistress in Greek mythology of the pride and strife of animal life (Fig. 56).[2]

[1] The symbol is too general and too dependent on the particular context for specific reference, but see C. G. Jung, *The Integration of the Personality* (Kegan Paul, French, Trubner, 1940), p. 103; Erich Neumann, *The Origins and History of Consciousness* (Routledge and Kegan Paul, 1954); Heinrich Zimmer, *Myths and Symbols in Indian Art and Civilisation* (Bollingen Foundation, 1946).

[2] See C. Kerenyi, *The Gods of the Greeks* (Thames and Hudson, 1951), pp. 145–7.

The radiant woman standing beside the man points upward towards the other, heavenly chariot, as well as down (Fig. 57). Notice that the folds of her veil and garment are lit partly by the mild radiance which seems to illumine her, and partly by the iridescent rainbow-colours reflecting from the sea; there is also a warm reflection from the crimson of the man's robe. She seems to reflect all these, rather than to have any colour herself. The waiting chariot above, to which she points, is man's higher self, or the higher human potential to which man is heir (Figs. 56 and 58). She points to his link with his higher nature and the supersensual life. There, above, his higher potentiality is asleep in the chariot. This figure in the chariot is nimbed and has a magnificent aura; he holds a sceptre in his right hand, but his head and features show him to be a replica of the man below. He is another aspect of the kneeling man, only he is reclined in sleep, as yet unawakened.

Similarly, the goddess of the waters is the counterpart of the radiant woman. Although she is now riding across the sea with her dark horses, she has descended from the skies where the other chariot waits, as is evident from the trail of cloudy vapours in her wake, which shows the course of her descent (Fig. 56).

We have here, therefore, four aspects of a totality, two male and two female. For this picture shows man placed between the light and dark aspects of life. The opposite poles of his nature are opened up in him: it is the perennial moment of crisis and the moment of its possible solution. Here is depicted, in these assembled images, the act of facing and accepting the forces which stand outside consciousness, and which in their height and depth beat upon his fragile personal life. In facing up to this, in accepting the dark and wild sea and the threatening form of the female goddess, he inducts its power, transforms its dynamic energy, and achieves a new and living synthesis. By this act of integration and regeneration, his sleeping counterpart above will be awakened, potentiality will become actuality, he will spring to life in his chariot drawn by the four superb horses, who are waiting to gallop away.

The radiant female is the medium by which this act is achieved;

she is also another, and a revealing aspect of it. As the man, by his act, awakens the heavenly charioteer, so she absorbs into herself the power and energy of the female charioteer careering over the waters. This goddess of nature is the dark aspect of the anima, with her animal impulses and drives. She is the energic, horrific aspect of life, kali, the fierce and destructive aspect of the Great Mother.[1] Representing the animal depths of man's soul, she reveals to him all the elemental reactions which succeed on each act of separateness to which he succumbs. She mirrors his contradictions and conflicts, for the primordial energy of his nature is drawn from her. Therefore she is the goddess of fear, and incipient in her are all the forms of the nightmare, of Hecate and witchcraft, of Echidna, mother of all horrors. All the distortions of man's nature can appear in her, as human records show.[2] But with the act of regeneration she becomes reintegrated with the radiant anima, the soul-figure whom Blake, in his later writing, called *Jerusalem*.

Regeneration is the meeting of consciousness with the primordial life forces, their acceptance and integration, and so their transformation. As shown here it is an act performed mid-way between the light kingdom, and the dark, prolific will of nature. Figuratively, it takes place on the brink of the outrageous sea, but in sight of heaven.

What, then, is the meaning of the right side of the picture and how does it fit in with the interpretation so far suggested? Perhaps the feature about this part of the picture which first demands explanation, because it is very indicative, is the fire which issues from the hill (Fig. 59). These flames are light and lambent above, but dark and angry below. Now fire seen in this way in dreams and visions shows a state of psychological crisis; the fire may indicate a

[1] For the Anima, see Jungian literature generally, especially C. G. Jung, op. cit., and *Two Essays in Analytical Psychology* (Routledge and Kegan Paul, 1954). For Kali, see Heinrich Zimmer, op. cit., especially pp. 211–15; also his *Kunstform und Yoga im Indischen Kultbild* (Berlin 1926). For visionary experiences of Kali (and for many other symbol-images) see that remarkable record of Ramakrishna's conversations: *The Gospel of Ramakrishna,* translated by Swami Nikhilananda (Sri Ramakrishna Math, Mylapore, Madras, 1947). See also E. Neumann, op. cit., part 1, sect. A, chap. 2: 'The Great Mother'.

[2] See C. G. Jung, *Psychology of the Unconscious* (Routledge and Kegan Paul, 1919).

state of extreme fear, but it can also have the meaning of immanent achievement and development. The fire of initiation and mission is sometimes seen in this way, in spontaneous vision, dream, or phantasy. In this picture, therefore, the fire certainly indicates a sense of psychological crisis, and reflects the dramatic act being performed on the sea-shore; for the light and dark aspects of life cannot confront each other in a man without there being a state of crisis, uncertainty, and flux. In this situation, the angry, red flames below, which issue from the steps and between the roots above the river, are the flames of hell, of unassuaged desire, torment, and suffering. All the fierceness of man's nature is expressed in this fire, which emanates from the unappeased passions and burning wills and desires, which are without apparent hope of assimilation with the good and reasonable. But on the hill above play the lighter lambent flames of dynamic life-energy. This fire is of a quite different character and is symptomatic of an altogether more integrated state. This is the fire which appears to those who have made contact with the mana-personality (to use the Jungian phrase).[1] Such were the flames which played around the burning bush, without consuming it, which Moses saw in vision; Moses, the prophet who was being called to his great mission. Swedenborg also saw such flames, and it is clear that Goethe was familiar with such fire from his repeated use of this symbol in the second part of *Faust*. Blake himself undoubtedly had many experiences of the vision of fire, as is amply apparent from his writing and paintings.[2] Here, in this picture, a third aspect of the fire symbol is shown. The radiant beams of light in the sky, which surround the waiting chariot, are of a still different order, as their colour and quality imply. These are the flaming lights of spiritual energy in which there is a release from individual will and separateness. The fire and flames, therefore, indicate not only psychological crisis, but three levels of possibility, all of which are present here.

On the hillside under the trees are weavers and spinners. Man's life is not creatively free; it contains a creative element, but it is also

[1] See his *Two Essays* (cited above).

[2] See *Note E*, p. 129.

essentially conditioned. So, his creative side can be considered as the warp which is interwoven continually with the many-coloured weft. In the process of weaving, the warp shapes the weft of every-day experience and from the two a pattern is for ever being woven. The weft can be taken as the conditioned and conditioning factors of life; the warp strung on the loom, as the creative, formative possibility of life. Whilst the warp controls the pattern and quality of the web, the weft, which represents the concrete facts of man's fate, is also an essential part of it and can by no means be ignored. The weavers and spinners here, as in all Blake's work, stand for this day-to-day process of living.[1] They are females, as they represent the given conditioned aspect of life with which man's formative side is in continual reaction. Hence the endless process of weaving and spinning, which is life. Moment by moment man's fate, his Karma, is playing out its role in conjunction with the creative possibility always latent in him.[2]

Thus, in this part of the picture, one is aware of an upward and downward movement. There is creative life becoming freer of entanglement, and there is downward-sinking life, becoming more and more involved and enmeshed. Moving upward is the woman on the steps carrying the bucket. This bucket is covered with scales, always an atavistic attribute; the water she is carrying has inferior and tainted associations. But above, in the paradisaical grove where the angelic figures move in procession, the vessels they carry on their heads may contain ambrosial liquor. The contrast between these beings and the rather equivocal female with the scaled bucket, is clearly suggested. Also, there is the creative process implied in the labours of the spinners and the weavers. But the downward movement is hinted at in the nixie reclining half-submerged in water, and the two figures on the right with their net. It is strongly emphasized in the writhing group of nudes, who are being carried down by the river's current, and whose struggles and contorted limbs and faces, express a state of torment.

[1] Blake sums up his weaving and spinning images in a stanza of incomparable insight at the end of *Milton* (plate 49, lines 7–15): 'I heard it named the Woof of Six Thousand Years.'

[2] Some specific references to weaving and spinning images in Blake's work are given later, under the Detailed Interpretation (right side of picture).

But most important of all, for the understanding of this side of the picture, is the river. The river is the archetypal symbol of the threshold. Every threshold has a positive and a negative aspect. The river threshold here, as always in like contexts, poses a dramatic and vital challenge. Can one cross the river and gain access to the fresh fields beyond, the steps, the hill, the paradisaical grove above? Or will one fall into it, be lured, or sucked under, to drown in the water, or perhaps be carried away by the current like the fearful group on the left? Can one, indeed, even summon the courage to make the attempt to cross? Such is always the symbolic meaning of the river as threshold symbol in dreams, myths, and fairy tales.

Here the river has its negative, threatening aspect, just as has the fire which issues from the hill. The water of this river is dark, and fear and foreboding is conveyed by the nixie and the net, which may fish up strange and uncouth things. The tormented group has been lured down the stream to its undoing. But the river also has its positive, inviting aspect. On the farther bank, the woman is ascending the lower steps carrying her bucket towards the angelic water-carriers in the grove above. The dark, atavistic waters of this stream, carried in the scaly bucket, may, if the ascent of the hill is accomplished, become the pure water of life, the water which is made wine. There is hope and promise suggested here, in the serenity of the angelic procession, and in the idyllic landscape which lies beyond the hill.

This right side of the picture, therefore, is an extended commentary on the dramatic act performed on the left. It introduces images and symbols which greatly expand the context of the principal theme, and which give weight and direction to its meaning. There is the fire symbol of psychological crisis, of mana energy, and of spiritual ecstasy; there is the threshold image of the river, and the water which can be transmuted into wine; and there are the weaving and spinning symbols of the process of day to day living.

One further aspect of this side of the picture still awaits notice (Fig. 59). It is framed by four trees, with a fifth just visible on the extreme right. These trees unite the earth with 'heaven'; they link the river of the threshold with the radiant light of the sky, and they frame the way of ascent and descent of human life which lies between. Yet there is a curious inverted emphasis expressed in these trees, which will hardly escape the notice of anyone who looks at the picture carefully. The green leaves, which merge with the canopy of the sky and are transparent with light, are far more firmly anchored in the firmament above than the sprawling roots below are grounded in the earth; the roots writhe and crawl on its surface without foundation and sustenance.[1] These trees receive their life and support from above, and not from below. Blake (who could draw firmly rooted trees when he wished to) is here giving expression to an archetypal symbol, which in seeming contradiction to the emphasis placed elsewhere in the picture on the acceptance of nature and the primordial forces of life, stresses the very opposite point of view. The trees do not grow up from the earth but down from the sky. They link heaven and earth, like the axle-tree of the world in the Germanic and Norse myths, but they are specifically upside-down trees like the Sephiroth Tree of the Kabbala, and the Tree of Hindu and Buddhist mythology. Both these mythical trees had their roots in the sky and their branches spread downwards into the world.[2] This paradoxical and compensatory point of view is very important in the total understanding of the picture. Above and below, light and dark, are relative terms. The consciousness which divides them and contrasts them must also learn how to reunite them in a comprehensive unity.[3]

DETAILED INTERPRETATION (LEFT SIDE)

Let us now look at this picture with detailed reference to Blake's known work, beginning with the left side where, as I have suggested, the central action takes place.

[1] Needless to say, Blake's trees generally are firmly rooted in the ground. The effect hereis undoubtedly intentional.

[2] See *Standard Dictionary of Folklore, Mythology and Legend* (Funk and Wagnall, New York, 1950) under 'Yggdrasil'. Also, Alan W. Watts, *Myth and Ritual in Christianity* (Thames and Hudson, 1953), pp. 159–60, 199.

[3] This same image is represented by Blake in the Preludium to *Europe*, in the text and illustration, where Vala is shown standing on her head: 'My roots are brandished in the heavens, my fruits on earth beneath.' See *Europe*, plate 4, Fitzwilliam Museum, Riches copy.

There can be little doubt that the man, in his double aspect of kneeling figure by the sea and asleep in his chariot above, represents Albion or Jesus (Fig. 56). Figure 60 shows a typical portrayal of Jesus from Blake's 'Paradise Regained' series, done in about 1808. Jesus here has the same rather small head, regular features, and short beard. Jesus is also represented in this way in the 'Paradise Lost' series of approximately the same date.

The idea that man as regards his higher potentiality is asleep is a basic one with Blake, which has already been alluded to (page 22). In *The Four Zoas* man's fall into a state of chaos is described as being due to his *renouncing the Divine Vision*. By *Turning his Eyes outward to Self, losing the Divine Vision*, he cut himself off from his higher aspect, his link with the divine, his totality.[1] In the Prophetic Book *Jerusalem*, Albion the Ancient Man, or archetypal man (of whom everyone is an individualized fraction), has fallen asleep, sunk down in the sleep of psychological death.[2] The aim of Blake's Prophetic Book is to show how psychological and spiritual harmony can be restored; when this is achieved Albion will awaken and arise in his majesty. *Heaven, Earth and Hell shall henceforth live in harmony*.[3] But meanwhile, until this is accomplished, Albion is divided from the *Eternal Great Humanity Divine. The Real Human* is left, as it were, sleeping above in Eternity, whilst individual man, as we know him, struggles in the resulting chaos of mundane life, which he calls the world of 'creation'.[4]

This same idea, which implies the possibility of reintegration and regeneration, colours many of Blake's shorter poems. It is specially noteworthy in *The Bard*, the poem which in several editions introduces the *Songs of Experience*. It is expressed most clearly of all, however, in the Prophetic Book *Milton*, and a few examples are

[1] *The Four Zoas*, book 1, lines 6–20: 'His fall into Division . . . His fall into the Generation of decay and death . . .' (lines 18–19); Book 1, lines 287–95; Book 2, lines 2–3 (quoted); Book 3, lines 37–43, &c.

[2] 'Albion was the Parent of the Druids: and in his Chaotic State of Sleep Satan and Adam and the whole World was created by the Elohim'; *Jerusalem*, plate 27, Prologue to chap. 2, 'To the Jews'.

[3] See *Note F*, p. 129.

[4] See the phrase used in *A Vision of the Last Judgment* (Keynes edition, vol. iii, p. 152): Albion 'in whose sleep or chaos creation began'.

worth quoting here. But it must always be remembered that this is an image or symbol, something which is beyond complete human comprehension: it is not an intellectual idea.

When Milton descends again to earth, to redeem his unresolved problems, a part of him is left above: *As one sleeping on a Couch of Gold*, a state, says Blake, like a man who dreams, but does not know whilst he is dreaming that his body is lying there asleep.[1] In another place Milton is described as living in three parts: (1) a self-righteous puritan part, (2) a struggling part, (3) a *Real Human* who walks above *in power and majesty*, though darkened.[2] Only when man re-establishes his link with the *Eternal Great Humanity*[3] does he again become a *Real Human*—this is Blake's fundamental theme.

Now this is quite clearly the theme alluded to in this picture. The *Real Human* is asleep on the *Couch of Gold* above, which is also a chariot. Man has fallen into a *Void outside of Existence*, that is, into a *sleep or chaos*.[4] This is the state in which 'creation' begins (the world as we know it), because *Error is created. Truth is Eternal.* For creation is a projection of the mind, illusion, maya—this is Blake's thought, as pointed out at the end of the previous chapter.

But this picture shows us the moment of integration, of regeneration. The regenerative act of self-sacrifice, acceptance, and assimilation will bring unity of being once more, and the chariot with the fiery steeds will be activated.

The chariot, with Blake, is always a symbol of spiritual energy. Figure 62 shows his colour print of Elisha receiving his mantel of prophecy from Elijah, who is about to ascend in his fiery chariot.[5] Like Elijah, the prophet who knew how to listen to and express his

[1] *Milton*, plate 17, lines 1–16.

[2] Ibid., plate 22, lines 7–41.

[3] Ibid., plate 33, lines 8–20.

[4] Ibid., plate 48, line 37 to plate 49, lines 1–2:

> 'Is this the Void Outside of Existence, which if entere'd into
> Becomes a Womb? and is this the Death Couch of Albion?'

Compare *Jerusalem*, Frontispiece, lines now erased where this phrase is again used; see Keynes edition, vol. iii, p. 409; see also the Trianon Press facsimile of *Jerusalem* (published for the Blake Trust, *c.* 1950).

[5] Colour print in the Tate Gallery.

intuitive, visionary power, Blake also summoned his spiritual vehicle:

> *O clouds unfold!*
> *Bring me my Chariot of fire!*[1]

In his poem the *Everlasting Gospel* Blake describes how Jesus, refusing to obey and conform to the Church religion of his day with its laws of sin and punishment:

> *Became a Chariot of fire.*
> *Throughout the land he took his course,*
> *And trac'd diseases to their source.*

Note again here the emphasis on the source of disease; that is, on uncovering the trouble, facing up to it, understanding it, and not blindly fighting it.

But what are the four horses harnessed to the chariot and painted by Blake with such superb feeling (Fig. 58)? Who are the female attendants grooming the horses and gathered round the chariot, some with musical instruments? The four horses represent the four Zoas, that is man's four different natures, or the four different aspects of human nature. These natures work through the four psychological functions, which can be regarded as their instruments. Blake named these four living creatures, or Zoas, which are referred to in the Apocalypse and in Ezekiel's vision, as follows: (1) Urizen, who corresponds with the rational, thinking, intellectual function; (2) Luvah, who is the feeling or emotional function; (3) Los, the intuitive function or imagination; (4) Tharmas, the function of sensation, or the body with its five sense organs and the basic sympathetic nervous system.

The four Zoas are harnessed like horses to the chariot, but unless they pull in harmony and subject to the charioteer there is disaster. The usurpation of will and power by one or other of the Zoas, that is, one or other of the psychological functions, is a principle theme of Blake's long Prophetic Book of that name, and is also repeated in

[1] Lines from 'Jerusalem', the lyric poem from the Prologue to *Milton* (Keynes edition, pp. 305–6).

many parts of *Milton* and *Jerusalem*. In a water-colour from the 'Paradise Lost' series (Fig. 61), showing the expulsion of Adam and Eve from Paradise, Blake shows how the four Zoas, in the form of four horsemen, accompanied man out of Eden. Needless to say, there is no mention of them in Milton's poem, such psychological images being far beyond the understanding of the rhetorical puritan poet. But it is only necessary here to allude briefly to the universality of this symbol of the 'Four living Creatures', as it has been extensively studied in Jungian literature, in connexion with the psychological functions. It can be traced in the Four Sons of Horus, the Vision of Ezekiel, the Four Beasts of the Evangelists; also in the four fixed Signs of the Zodiac; and in Hindu and Buddhist mythology in the Caryatid Kings, the regents of the four quarters.[1]

The female attendants, and the sylphic female forms, some with musical instruments, attendant on the sleeper in his chariot (Fig. 56), are the *Daughters of Beulah*—one of Blake's most penetrating and wonderful symbolic images. They have already been briefly discussed with reference to plate 25 of *Jerusalem*, in connexion with Picture 16 of *The Gates of Paradise* (pp. 51–52). *The Daughters of Beulah* are the archetypal symbols, or more accurately, man's power of apprehending things through symbols. Without the medium of the image or symbol, which speaks as much to man's unconscious side as to his conscious mind, he could never awaken, never re-establish his link with the *Real Human* who sleeps above. Seen from the reverse point of view, the task of the *Daughters of Beulah* is *to feed the sleepers on their couches*;[2] that is to say, they are always there, as certain as eternity itself, and will be found ministering to man's psychological and spiritual needs by anyone who can learn to perceive them.

In that moment of crisis and realization in *Milton*, when the

[1] For the four Zoas, apart from the works mentioned, see Blake's comment about them in *A Vision of the Last Judgment* (Keynes edition, p. 155); S. Foster Damon, *William Blake, his Philosophy and Symbols* (New York, 1947), pp. 145; W. P. Wittcutt, *Blake, a psychological study* (Hollis and Carter, 1946), the earlier chapters of this book are a brilliant psychological interpretation on Jungian lines; C. G. Jung, *Psychological Types* (Routledge and Kegan Paul, 1923); Alan W. Watts, op. cit., pp. 38, 161.

[2] See *Milton*, plate 30, lines 44–63.

Spectre, or separate self, is seen for what it is and is thereby overthrown, they are shown as present with their instruments of music (Fig. 25).[1] They appear, too, on several of the early pages of *Jerusalem* in similar aspect as here. Blake's clearest account of the Beulah image is, perhaps, that given in plate 33 of *Milton*, whilst in his poem 'The Crystal Cabinet', he defines the limitations of the symbol, which like all media of knowledge, is a relative thing only. Blake clearly thought it important to remember this fact too.

It may perhaps be questioned whether the nimbed figure asleep in the chariot in the sky is not in some way connected with the sun-god, Apollo, of Greek mythology. It is worth considering this before proceeding farther. For Blake there was an inner aspect of the sun, as well as an outer physical one. The image of the sun apparent to introverted vision was no less real for Blake than the external image, which is seen by the sense organs of sight. Indeed the inner sun, in its symbolic and spiritual quality, was by far the more important and real of the two for Blake, and it is undoubtedly this aspect which he depicts here in this picture. Los is described as *a Terrible flaming Sun* in the vision recorded and illustrated in *Milton*, already referred to (Fig. 47, see pp. 47–48).[2] In the poem which begins *With happiness stretch'd across the hills,* which he sent to his friend Butts from Felpham in November 1802—a poem which is particularly revealing of Blake's mind and the working of his intuitive understanding—he characteristically insists on this difference:

> *Then Los appear'd in all his power:*
> *In the Sun he appear'd, descending before*
> *My face in fierce flames; in my double sight*
> *Twas outward a Sun, inward Los in his might.*

The difference is exactly that described in modern psychological terminology as introverted and extraverted vision, or attitude.

Further, there are two direct statements of Blake about this, one recorded by Henry Crabb Robinson, the other recorded in Blake's

[1] *Milton,* plate 15 (British Museum copy).
[2] Ibid., plate 24 (British Museum copy, plate 27).

own Notebook. The former is Blake's statement to the incredulous Crabb Robinson (an acquaintance of his latter days) that he had once seen the Spiritual Sun on Primrose Hill. 'You never saw the Spiritual Sun (said Blake). I have. I saw him on Primrose Hill. He said, Do you take me for the Greek Apollo? "No", I said, "That (pointing to the sky), that is the Greek Apollo. He is Satan".'[1] (Again, there could be no clearer differentiation than this between extraverted and introverted vision.) The second statement is as follows:

'I assert for My Self that I do not behold the outward Creation and that to me it is hindrance and not Action; it is as the dirt upon my feet, No part of Me. "What", it will be questioned, "When the Sun rises, do you not see a round disk of fire somewhat like a Guinea?" O no, no, I see an Innumerable company of the Heavenly host crying, "Holy, Holy, Holy is the Lord God Almighty." I question not my Corporeal or Vegetative Eye any more than I would question a Window concerning a Sight. I look thro' it and not with it.'[2]

Now let us follow down in the wake of the chariot driven by the woman across the sea—for this also is a manifestation of the Eternal Unity.

This woman is Vala, the goddess of Nature, with her instinctive urges and animal drives and impulses. The Prophetic Book now known as *The Four Zoas* was originally entitled *Vala*, and its opening line begins: *The Song of the Aged Mother which shook the heavens with Wrath.* For Vala was for Blake the mother-goddess, identified with nature and the conditioned, female side of life, thus in eternal opposition to heaven, the formative male side, as emphasized in this line (the heaven of consciousness being enraged at her incomprehensible 'otherness').[3] A little later in *The Four Zoas* there is a Song of Death, which is also called a *Song of Vala*; its

[1] See Arthur Symons, *William Blake*, part ii (which records extracts from the Diary of Henry Crabb Robinson), p. 291 (Constable, 1907).

[2] Keynes edition, vol. iii, p. 162 (p. 95 of MS.).

[3] S. Foster Damon, op. cit., pp. 364–5, suggested that the name 'Vala' was derived from Scandinavian mythology. N. Frye, *Fearful Symmetry*, p. 270, repeats this. But this derivation is denied by H. M. Margoliouth, *William Blake's Vala* (Oxford, 1956), p. xviii, who suggests a derivation from 'veil'.

theme is an account of how the conditioned, Yin side of life has usurped the place of the formative Yang side, just as in the myth of Adam's fall and Eve's usurpation of power, as previously explained (pp. 22–23). Here also there is a reference to *the Fallen Man* who *takes his repose.*[1] For these reasons it is called a Song of Death, as the two following quotations emphasize:

> *I have refused to look upon the Universal Vision . . .*
> *Refusing to behold the Divine Vision which all behold*
> *And live thereby, he is sunk down into a deadly sleep.*[2]

Towards the end of *The Four Zoas* there is an account of Vala in her most sinister aspect:

> *A False Feminine Counterpart of Lovely Delusive Beauty . . .*
> *Vala, drawn down into a Vegetated body, now triumphant.*[3]

She is exalted by Satan, clothed in scarlet and gold and bejewelled, and on her forehead is inscribed 'Mystery'. This is the complete inversion of the dark female principle, which can only be redeemed by sacrificing itself to the transmuting power of the light.

In the Arlington Court picture, Vala, riding over the sea with her horses, represents the dark, surging, animal side of man's life; she is the threatening, uncontrolled power of the unconscious, the dark anima. Unless man's relationship with her is right, she appears fearful and threatening to him, the feminine counterpart of Satan.[4] But here, in the picture, she is seen in her true aspect. She is the powerful goddess of night, as opposed to the god of day. Yet she is just as real, just as essential as he is, for both are but two aspects of one incomprehensible whole. So here she wears the lunar horns of Artemis. In the *Illustrations of the Book of Job,* Blake used this Artemis-like goddess to represent the dark, lunar, animal side of life, as opposed to the light, masculine, Apollonian sun-god of day

[1] See *The Four Zoas,* book 1, lines 257–77.

[2] Lines 271; 287–8.

[3] Book 8, lines 265–94.

[4] See *Milton,* plate 43, lines 9–14:

> 'The Spectre of Satan stood upon the roaring sea and beheld
> Milton within his sleeping Humanity. . . .'

(Fig. 63). In this fourteenth plate of the Job illustrations, Apollo and Artemis are used as complimentary figures or symbols. For in this engraving these two aspects of life are shown in their right relationship one with another; it is the moment of harmony and unitive vision, 'When the Morning Stars sang together and all the Sons of God shouted for joy'. This also is the moment heralded here in the Arlington picture of Regeneration.

But there is more to say about this important image of the dark anima, Vala. The two small figures who have gone out into the sea to meet Vala in her chariot (Fig. 56) are Los and Enitharmon (or so I should like to suggest). Los is man's intuitive, imaginative faculty in its formative aspect; Enitharmon, Los's female counterpart, or *emanation*, is intuition, or imagination, in its empirical aspect. Los is always beside man to guide him; he strives to rescue the prostrate, schizophrenic Albion (Fig. 40; see pp. 40–41); he even enters Death's Door with him (Fig. 35, see pp. 33–34), as we have already seen. Here he is with him again, at this crucial moment, and by an imaginative act he has gone out into the sea of the unconscious with Enitharmon to find a way of reconciliation with Vala. What is the meaning of this, and what grounds are there for interpreting these two small personages in this way?

In *The Four Zoas* it is recounted how Luvah and Vala are reborn as the children of Los and Enitharmon.[1] Luvah represents man's feeling or emotional function, Vala (who is his counterpart or *emanation*) his instinctive, animal nature. The story in Blake's myth describes a process of psychological degeneration, or aberration. Los, *infected, mad, shrunk into fixed space* with Enitharmon; they petrify. From Los and Enitharmon in this degenerate state are born Luvah and Vala as the *fiery child*, red Orc. That is, Orc (aggression) is the libido manifesting in a personality where there is some degree of disturbance and conflict. The myth continues with the story of the rearing of Orc and recounts the Oedipus situation, for Orc *the ruddy boy* embraces his mother and excites Los's jealousy,

[1] *The Four Zoas*, book 3, lines 14–23 (where it is foretold); book 5, lines 23–65 (where it is recounted); lines 70–142 for the rearing of Orc.

who moreover perceives murderous intentions against himself in Orc. For Orc is a degenerate form of Luvah (love) whose birth is described as the result, or manifestation, of a fallen state. But were regeneration possible, then the psychological functions would again work in harmony, and the natural man would cease to be at enmity with the spiritual.

Here, then, in the picture (so I would suggest) Blake is expressing the idea that Los and Enitharmon (intuition) already perceive, or dimly recognize in the unconscious depths, that Vala, the dark, fierce goddess of instinctive animal life, can be regenerated through Luvah, and so assimilated and reintegrated in the new man who is struggling for unity and rebirth.[1]

But the important point about the transformation of Vala is that it is through man's feeling side, through Luvah, that the instincts are regenerated. In Blake's mythology, Vala is the feminine counterpart of Luvah; that is, man's instinctive, animal nature is a part of, or aspect of, his feeling, or emotional nature. It is human feeling and emotion which complete and give meaning to the former. Now the man kneeling by the sea, Albion or Jesus, is clothed in *Luvah's Robe of Blood*. This is certainly the meaning of the crimson robe which he wears. *Luvah's Robe of Blood* is a very important image in Blake's writing, used both in *The Four Zoas* and *Milton*; it signifies the suffering and compassion of the man of feeling.[2] The development of feeling is just as important as the development of the intellect; for unless a man is sensitive and fully alive and open to the whole range of his emotional nature, he remains a barbarian at heart. Ruthlessness is the characteristic of the barbarian. But the sensitive man has great discrimination of feeling, and this is something quite different from intellectual and logical discrimination.

To illustrate this point we may recall how it has been said that

[1] Parallels to this can be found in Hindu and Vedanta mythology. Compare the verse of Ramprasad:

'. . . the Mother (Kali) lives in all bodies,
See, O dazzled and deluded eye, even in the dark the Mother (Kali) is the light of the dark.'

Quoted in H. Zimmer, *Kunstform und Yoga*, p. 141.

[2] For example, *The Four Zoas*, book 1, lines 357–63; book 2, lines 247–64. *Milton*, plate 49, lines 7–15.

Christianity, with its strong appeal to the emotions, brought a sense of humanity to the late Roman empire and its barbarian conquerors. Christianity, with its stress on compassion and the value of feeling, was able gradually to educate and refine post-classical and early medieval Europe. It is just the same with the individual. It is only through the development of his feeling-side that he can educate and mature his instinctive, unconscious life. The *Robe of Blood* signifies accepting the experience, but bringing to it the sensibility and discrimination of feeling, which entails suffering. The blood of suffering, of the felt-through experience, of sacrifice, must be shed. Nor must this be an intellectual, or theoretical process only; it must be played out in actuality for it to have any meaning.

Therefore, unless man's feeling side is highly developed, the price of redeeming the unconscious cannot be paid. For the act of integration and regeneration to be possible, man must be clothed in his *Robe of Blood*. Instinctive, animal nature is only transformed through feeling, and only then can Vala become one with Luvah; which means that the dark anima then becomes indistinguishable from the light.

The scene of the act of redemption and regeneration is the seashore. This threshold between land and sea is symbolic of the meeting of the conscious and unconscious, of the generative and formative aspects of life. In *Milton* Blake makes use of this symbol, which has great power in the unconscious, in a remarkable picture (Fig. 64).[1] At the foot of a cliff, on the rocks which are washed by the sea, lie a man and woman in sexual union. This is a picture of generation, the physical example of the fructifying union of the two different and opposite aspects of human life, the male and female. Over this union hovers the eagle of vision. For man's divided being can attain to unity, and this can be realized in a way which transcends the physical example of it. Generation is the prototype of regeneration, and the latter implies *resurrection to Unity*.[2]

We now come to the radiant female who stands beside the kneeling man and occupies the centre of the picture (Fig. 57). The whole

[1] British Museum copy, plate 38.

[2] *The Four Zoas*, plate 1, lines 18–20.

process of the act of regeneration is expressed in her. She points both down and up, signifying the reconciliation of the 'above' and the 'below', of heaven and earth. This is the admonitory gesture seen in many images of Buddha, particularly in Chinese sculpture of the Wei and succeeding dynasties.

This figure represents Jerusalem, the name used in Blake's later work for the symbol of man's regenerate nature, which exists always as a possibility for him. Here she stands waiting—both as the medium of the regenerative act Albion is about to achieve, and as his reward, that is the fruition of the regenerate life itself. She is the means of the unification of his unredeemed nature, and when this is accomplished she will contain within herself all the power and energy of his Vala nature. This is beautifully expressed in the picture by the reflection of the many colours in her iridescent veil and garment.

Blake's symbols for the various aspects of the unconscious are very subtle and varied. He experienced the unconscious as a female, and he saw that this female image had both a light and a dark aspect. Vala is the dark, energic, threatening side of the unconscious; she is also its horrific aspect. This is the reason for the fear expressed in the opening lines of *Vala, or The Four Zoas:*

The heavens quake, the earth was moved and shudder'd, and the mountains
With all their woods, the streams and valleys wail'd in dismal fear.

Jerusalem, on the other hand, is the light aspect of the unconscious, seen as source of life-value and inspiration; she is the image of the soul, man's ideal, his guiding star and eternal beloved. This is the light anima of Jungian psychology. As such she is shown here, the radiant, iridescent female. It is worth comparing this representation of her with Los's vision of Jerusalem, illustrated in plate 14 of *Jerusalem*, and already alluded to (Fig. 36; see p. 35). There she is shown as the hopeful, inspiring vision of the ideal.

But Blake realized that these two aspects of the unconscious are fundamentally one. In *Jerusalem*, plate 18 (Fig. 65), Vala and Jerusalem are shown as both springing from the same source—their feet touch—though they are both reaching out in opposite directions. They are two diverging aspects of one thing.

Man, in the chaotic and contradictory state of fallen Albion, is always refusing, repressing, condemning one aspect of the unconscious, whilst inviting the other. Jerusalem is rejected, Vala is encouraged. But this leads to confusion and conflict. The story of this takes up a large part of the Prophetic Book *Jerusalem*. On plate 32 this situation is illustrated (Fig. 66). Here the one aspect is darkened and veiled, the other is cherished with her children.

This problem of the anima, the relation between a man's consciousness and the unconscious, Blake treated at great length in one of his earlier Prophetic Books, *The Visions of the Daughters of Albion*. This is the problem as encountered by the young man long before middle age. Plate 1 from this poem (Fig. 67) shows Oothoon, as the repressed anima is there called, back to back with Bromion, who is the physical, carnal side of man, who desires her, but cannot satisfy her. But Oothoon herself is rejected by Theotormon, the pious, pseudo-religious character in man. In plate 7 (Fig. 68)[1] she haunts Theotormon as a disturbing influence. But she is chained by one foot. The pious idealist is bereaving himself of the true source of life. Nor can a man have one aspect of the anima if he represses and renounces the other.

None the less the situation between consciousness and the repressed unconscious can grow much worse than this. In plate 26 of *Jerusalem* (Fig. 71), Blake shows the rationalistic, materialistic man *Hand* repelling the anima still further. He stands with arms stiffly extended, a prey to the contradictions of the dualistic world of his restricted rationalism. He has long since forgotten how to listen to the voices of his own unconscious. He has sought to control it, or to disregard and repress it. Now it is burning him like the flames of hell in which he is tormented. He has his back to the anima, from whom alone can come the unifying, redeeming process which may save him. Repelled, cowed, long-since unheard, Jerusalem, his anima, cannot now even approach him.

[1] Both illustrations are taken from versions at the Tate Gallery.

Finally there comes the dangerous, schizoid state in which the anima, in her light aspect, becomes deeply buried in the unconscious; she is excluded from all contact with life. This is illustrated on plate 33 of *Jerusalem* (Fig. 40). The conscious ego, self-sufficient in pride and self-will, has become transformed into a frightful batlike vulture which hovers over the prostrate soul-figure. Man's Spectre, his ego, has become so inflated that it now divides him in two, cutting off his own source of inner life and light. Above, in a state of collapse, is Albion, personifying the individual who has fallen into this schizoid state; but Los is still with him, bending over him, caring for him, although the situation is now desperate.

All this is explained at great length in *Jerusalem*. A particularly interesting commentary on this psychological situation is afforded by an image of Blake's expressed in the myth of the *Veil of Vala*. Although it entails a slight digression it is relevant here, because of the net hanging in the river at the bottom right-hand corner of the Arlington Court picture (Figs. 54, 59).

The *Veil of Vala* first appears in the early Prophetic Book *Europe* in the form of a spider's web; it is shown in *Europe*, plate 12 (Fig. 33).[1] This is the web of moral virtue which man's dualistic view of life has projected on to his own nature. He becomes divided from himself, as he really is, by this projected web, or net, which emanates from his rigidly held moral code. In *Jerusalem* this net is found covering not only Vala, but also Jerusalem; for man has placed moral principles between his conscious attitudes and his unconscious life in all its aspects. Condemning, approving, justifying, he can no longer see life as it actually is; he can no longer experience it directly. His anima in both its aspects is veiled from him, or, as it were, covered by a web or net. Then, finally, it is recounted how Albion, ridden with feelings of guilt, and in desperation, casts the net away into the Atlantic (*Jerusalem*, plate 23):

He drew the Veil of Moral Virtue, woven for Cruel Laws
And cast it into the Atlantic Deep, to catch the Souls of the Dead.

[1] British Museum copy. It is there called Enitharmon's web.

This episode is illustrated on plate 24 of *Jerusalem* (Fig. 69). Pictorially, Blake expresses the idea as the female principal cast out on to the waters, where it appears as a sort of ark. But both Jerusalem and Vala were in the net. Both have now been cast out. In trying to root out one side of his life he has thrown away his better part as well.

Referring back now to the Arlington Court picture, this is the clue to the meaning of the net hanging in the water on the right side of the picture (Fig. 59). Thrown out—that is, the struggle of understanding and assimilation having been given up—the net vegetates *Knot by Knot, Day by Day*, and petrifies *among the Roots*.[1] It becomes part of the *Mundane Shell* and has to be remodelled by Los to become once more a substance capable of redemption and awakening. Here, then, the net hanging in the water is the moral law of right and wrong. It may catch the souls of the dead in the toils of its morality, and perhaps engender in the very immature a livelier sense of the conflict of 'good and evil'. But it has no meaning for the souls of the living, those who have already come to recognize the absolute relativity of all ideas of 'right and wrong'. For the living are 'breakers of nets'.[2] They are the prophets and enlightened men who go beyond the conventional morality of the day; they are those who have bathed in the flames of the mana-personality. They have realized the eternal limitation, and the ultimate stagnation, of trying to live by a rule. This approximation to a standard, and conforming to a superimposed pattern, is not life: it is the *Sleep of Ulro*. It is spiritual death about which it is said: *O that death and annihilation were the same*. But life is found only in the flowering process of total experience; and this entails *the passage through Eternal Death*, which is the only way to *the awakening to Eternal Life*.[3]

This diversion, and the illustrations concerned with Jerusalem and Vala, may have helped to show the complex nature of the rela-

[1] *Jerusalem*, plate 24, lines 61–62; plate 59, lines 2–4.

[2] 'It is so with Swedenborg: he shows the folly of Churches, and exposes hypocrites, till he imagines that all are religious, and himself the single one on earth that ever broke a net' (*Marriage of Heaven and Hell*, Keynes edition, p. 193). Compare W. B. Yeats's poem 'Into the Twilight': 'Come clear of the nets of right and wrong'.

[3] Quotations from *Jerusalem*, plate 4 (chap. 1); and plate 23, line 40.

tionship between consciousness and the many aspects of the unconscious, which appears as 'other' from it, just as darkness does from light. This is a theme which Blake never tired of exploring, and which he studied with quite extraordinary insight. When, therefore, Blake shows the radiant Jerusalem as here, full of the promise of the *Divine Vision and Fruition*, it is no mere trite and pious idea which he is expressing. Behind this visionary image, so simply portrayed in the Arlington Court picture, there is a mass of observation and comment. Blake well understood the significance of the supreme moment when Jerusalem will absorb Vala into herself. He illustrated the uniting of man and his soul-image in conjunction with the image of the lotus flower in plate 28 of *Jerusalem* (Fig. 70). The many forces of life in man take on a transcending unity, like the flowering lotus, the Living Flower which rises out of the murky depths.

SYMBOLIC STRUCTURE OF THE PICTURE

Before beginning the detailed interpretation of the right side of the picture, it is worth pausing for a moment to consider the basic symbolic structure of the Arlington Court picture as a whole. For it is built on principles which always express themselves alike among different peoples and at different times and places. Always, it is another glimpse of the same archetypal pattern of reality.

The theme of the picture is the light and dark aspects of life and their reconciliation. Both aspects contain their own animating, life-giving principles. Vala personifies the power of the dark side, whilst Jerusalem shines as man's guiding star. Man himself has his transcendental aspect as well as his individual, corporate existence struggling in day-to-day life.

The simplest symbolic expression of the duality of light and dark, which emerges from, and is contained in, an all-embracing unity, is the ancient Chinese symbol of the T'ai-chi, or the Great One (Fig. 72). Unity is represented as a circle or globe; a sinuous changing line divides the sphere into a light and a dark half. There is in each half an eye, or sperm, or nucleus, which represents its activating principle. As each half develops, the one now becomes two, the Yang and the Yin, and out of them develop 'the ten thousand things', that is, the endless chain of phenomenal existences. But Tao leads the philosopher back again from the multiplicity of phenomena to the Great One.

The example of the T'ai-chi here illustrated, is taken from a Taoist priest's robe; arranged round the T'ai-chi are the Eight Trigrams. These trigrams, which can be combined together into sixty-four hexagrams, are the basis of the 'I-Ching', the 'Book of Changes', which from time immemorial has provided the Chinese with a method of studying life from the point of view of the continual flux and change of things, which obey the laws of Yin and Yang, issue from the Great One, and always return to it and are contained within it.[1] This, stated briefly, is exactly the method and procedure of Blake in his Prophetic Books and in his art. Unless this is clearly understood it is very difficult to follow his meaning or appreciate his aims. His symbols, and the names of his mythical personages, cannot be tied down and tabulated, except in the most general and hypothetical way; for they are always changing according to the laws of enantiodromia. The whole purpose of his invented names and personages is to keep this flux of meaning ever ebbing and flowing. But so foreign has this idea become to modern Western thought (though no longer so to some of its more advanced sections) that much of Blake has remained quite unnecessarily obscure and misunderstood. Change, in the world of 'creation', is the essential of experience. The laws of change are far more important for anyone who is concerned with his relationship with the Great One, than are the laws of cause and effect, and similar logical constructions. This principle is the essence of Blake's 'prophetic' work in verse and pictures.[2]

When Blake conceives 'Michael and the Dragon' (Fig. 73) as interlocked in continually revolving struggle, he is expressing an

[1] For the *I-Ching*, see *The I-Ching or Book of Changes*, translated by Richard Wilhelm (Routledge and Kegan Paul, 1951), 2 vols.

[2] See *Note G*, p. 129.

image which has the same archetypal origin as a symbol such as the T'ai-chi. Michael and the Dragon, 'heaven' and 'hell', the light and dark principles (the one with the key, the other with the chain in this design), are locked in combat. There can be no victory, no solution within this circle, so long as the struggle remains on this same level; for the opposites are part of the essential structure of 'creation'. The *contraries are positives*, as Blake affirms. The strife of the contraries can only be 'redeemed' by an act which takes place (as it were) on a higher dimension.[1]

In the Arlington Court picture Blake has shown the light and dark principles manifesting in their various pairs of opposites, always linked by means of an intermediary third. The man on the sea-shore strives to reconcile the sea chariot with the heavenly chariot. The radiant female, Jerusalem, points to the need to reconcile man's earthly with his heavenly nature. Three aspects of man are shown; his potential union with the divine, his mundane individuality struggling in life, and his tormented form in the guise of the horned male struggling in the river. On the right side of the picture, the women are all grouped in threes (the tormented group in the river includes the horned male, whose significance will be explained later: pp. 85–87, Fig. 55). Three is the number of becoming, of effort, struggle with and through experience; it implies the forward-moving process of time. Four is the number of psychic structure, of being as opposed to becoming, of psycho-somatic totality. In this picture, the stable, structural parts show the number four. There is the quaternity with which we started—two aspects of the man, two of the female; there are the four horses representing the four psychological functions; the steps on the right are in flights of four; the trees which frame this side of the picture emphasize quaternity. There are also four rivers shown, the four rivers of Paradise, as will be explained later. (These remarks on numbers must, of course, be taken psychologically, and not mystically or

[1] See Chapter I, pp. 38–39, fig. 38. For an analogy to the 'higher dimension' metaphor, see *Jerusalem*, plate 36, penultimate lines: 'but the Divine Mercy | Steps beyond and redeems man in the body of Jesus.'

esoterically; they represent a means of apprehending things which is archetypal, and they can be experienced experimentally by anyone who has the interest and aptitude.)

These same principles can be found expressed in a very remarkable diagram drawn by Jacob Boehme, the Silesian shoemaker and mystic, who lived in the early seventeenth century, mostly before the outbreak of the Thirty Years War. The diagram illustrates one of his books, *The Forty Questions*, and is called the 'Philosophic Globe', or the 'Wonder Eye of Eternity' (Fig. 74).[1] Boehme explains in this book a great deal by means of the diagram, which contains so many fundamental ideas. Here I can only draw attention to one or two relevant points.

The two half circles are really spheres, or globes, which interlock. The dark sphere contains the 'wrathful' principle of God the Father. The light sphere contains the principle of the Spirit. The two spheres are contained within a greater sphere, and a square or quaternity is indicated outside this by the four principles marked in the four corners: Law, Self (on the dark side); Gospel, Resignation (on the light side). Connecting the centres of the light and dark spheres and dividing their peripheries is a cross: this is where the Son performs his perennial act, mid-way between the light and dark principles. Boehme, in his treatise and diagram, is clearly explaining in a more metaphysical way an insight into the nature of things similar to that which Blake is attempting in his picture. The principles of the trinity and the quaternity are clearly apparent in both; and so is the divine mystery of redemption, or regeneration.

DETAILED INTERPRETATION (RIGHT SIDE)

Turning now to the right side of the picture, let us begin with the river in the foreground (Fig. 59). The symbolic role of a river as a psychological threshold is emphasized in the Bible story of the

1 Jacob Boehme, *The Forty Questions of the Soul and The Clavis*. A modern edition, which reproduces the diagram, was published by John M. Watkins (1911), p. 45. The diagram is entitled: 'The Figure of the Philosophic Globe', or 'Eye of the Wonders of Eternity', or 'Looking Glass of Wisdom'.

Israelites escaping from Egypt and marching towards the Promised Land. First there was the miraculous crossing of the Red Sea; then, after the wilderness, the crossing of the river Arnon, the southern boundary between Israel and Moab. Next came Jordan, crossed near Gilgal, where the stones were set up to commemorate another miraculous crossing.[1] Each time the symbolic meaning of the crossing is stressed. Blake also used the river as a threshold symbol of decision and choice in a great deal of his writing, often with reference to the Bible names. This is particularly noticeable in *Milton*, perhaps the most autobiographical of all his Prophetic Books. A great part of the psychological action of the poem takes place on the river Arnon, the river of the Israelite epic.

To quote four examples from *Milton*: First, a river is mentioned as the place of trial, contention and strife of the three classes of mankind, the Elect, the Redeemed, and the Reprobate. *Thus they weep upon the fatal brook of Albion's River.*[2] Second, it is upon the river Arnon that Milton strives with Urizen, his rational and dogmatic mind: *Urizen rose and met him on the shores of Arnon and by the streams of the brooks.*[3] As he struggles there with Urizen, gaining the mastery for a minute, Albion rises and attempts to wade out into the deep, but is too weak and sinks down again. Then: *Urizen faints in terror striving among the brooks of Arnon.*[4] Third, it is there also that Milton is enticed by Rahab and Tirzah, who may loosely be regarded as representing sensuality and repression.[5] Fourthly, it is also there that the Five Females (sense organs) and the *Shadowy Mother* lure the sleepers *down the River Storge* (*which is Arnon*) *into the Dead Sea.*[6]

This river, the Arnon, Storge, Pison, or Albion's brook, is connected with crisis, and in this picture it speaks of the psychological and spiritual crisis which is here enacted. If we can cross the river we can begin to move upwards, with the woman who is carrying the bucket of water. At this stage the water is still polluted, brackish,

[1] Exod. xiv, Deut. iii, Joshua iii and iv.
[2] *Milton*, plate 14, line 35.
[3] Ibid., plate 21, lines 1–5.
[4] Ibid., plate 44, lines 32–53.
[5] Ibid., plate 21, lines 27–60, &c.
[6] Ibid., plate 38, lines 24–31.

as the scales which mark the bucket signify; for scales are an atavistic attribute. The woman, also, closely resembles in her posture and the curious webbed marking of her dress, the ministrant female at the banquet offered to Jesus by the Tempter, in the 'Paradise Regained' water-colour (Fig. 43). But on top of the hill there is every indication that the water is entirely different. It is carried in beautiful tall vessels with flaring rims on the heads of angelic figures, winged, and walking in harmonious procession. This is the water which is made wine, the living water of life, one of Blake's dearest images:

Then shall we return and see
The worlds of happy Eternity.
And throughout all Eternity
I forgive you, you forgive me.
As our dear Redeemer said:
'This the Wine, and this the Bread'.[1]

Immediately beneath the grove, where the transformed water is being carried, are a pair of river gods, with another one beyond, pouring their streams. There is a third stream with its reclining figure lower down towards the sea, on a terrace in the idyllic landscape immediately above the classical temple. These are three of the four Rivers of Paradise, often mentioned in Blake's writing. Where is the fourth? It is none other than the Pison, Arnon, or Albion's brook, the place of trial in the foreground of the picture. For this river too can be transformed into the pure waters of the rivers of Paradise.

Yet, in the picture, this river remains a place into which one may fall, or into which one may be lured. Nixies and syrens dwell there, and it is their custom to entice men under water and drown them.[2] Psychologically speaking, nixies and syrens indicate the attractive

[1] The last lines of the poem 'My Spectre around me night and day'. Compare *A Vision of the Last Judgment* (Keynes edition), vol. iii, p. 156, and many places in *Milton* and *Jerusalem.*

[2] Jung quotes Goethe (*Integration of the Personality*, p. 73):

'Halb zog sie ihn
Halb sank er hin
Und ward nicht mehr gesehen'.

power of the repressed anima. This is the meaning of the woman or nixie half-submerged and reclining on the tub or culvert in the right bottom corner of the picture. That Blake realized this psychological meaning of the submerged, or half submerged, female is clearly shown in plate 15 of *America* (Fig. 76). There Oothoon, the soul-figure or anima, is shown submerged and preyed on by fish and other primitive forms of life, which nourish themselves on her. Tyranny and oppression still dominate America from Europe; only when America is free will the anima emerge from the waters.

We must now look at the group of four writhing figures in the left foreground (Fig. 55), who are being *lured down the River Storge* (*which is Arnon*) *into the Dead Sea*. This group consists of three females and one horned male. The significance of this male figure is important and it must be elucidated. The Arlington Court picture, taken as a whole, shows the act of accepting the dark, unconscious side of life, and so resolving and redeeming it. This is also the theme of *Milton*, for Milton must learn how to see and accept all that lies in the shadow-side of life. A vision of this finally appears to Milton and it is personified as the female *Ololon*. Ololon represents the unresolved conflicts of his unconscious and she is a multiple female.[1] Blake explains of this multiple female:

> *They could not step into Vegetable Worlds without becoming*
> *The enemies of Humanity, except in a female Form.*[2]

The unconscious in its repressed aspect, perceived as a female, is a friend; at least, when the image is female it indicates a situation where a solution can still be found. As a male it is an enemy; as such it represents a far more complicated and intractible problem.[3] Now here, in this tormented group, there is a male. This is an allusion to the Red Dragon of Blake's *Vision of the Last Judgment*. In his

[1] See *Milton*, plate 49, lines 3–6.

[2] Ibid., plate 40, lines 13–20.

[3] This statement must be taken with reservation, but I believe it contains an important psychological truth. There are, of course, many benign male images (such as the Puer Eternus, Wise Old Man, &c.) but these do not represent the repressed unconscious, or the shadow, which is what I understand Blake to mean.

Notes on a lost version of this picture he explains that the Red Dragon is the Male-female, the female hidden in a male.[1] In the Petworth picture of the Last Judgment this monster with ten horns and seven heads is shown below the female Harlot Babylon. The indication is that the tormented group has sunk into the intractable Satanic state, which because it is something inverted, bears the stamp of irredeemable evil, or at least what appears to mortals to be beyond the pale of the opposites.

The rope, which this group holds, is a negative aspect of the thread of life; the thread leads to liberation, but the rope enmeshes and binds fast. The hank of rope which the horned man holds is drawn here in the same way as the hank of thread held by Enitharmon in the last plate of *Jerusalem* (Fig. 77).[2] There the thread has a positive connotation. The meaning of the rope, which indicates a great deal about the fate which is overtaking this downward-moving group, is connected with the *Tree of Mystery*. In his poem, *The Human Abstract*, one of the *Songs of Experience*, Blake explains the essential idea about the Tree of Mystery: it is the repressed unconscious wish, which is projected in a substitute and disguised form. It springs from a displaced and rationalized affect. This is the secret root not only of hypocrisy and self-deception, but of the whole world of 'illusion', as this word is used in Buddhism. It springs up from the smallest seed and grows rapidly into a great tree. It is one of the subtlest and most difficult psychological phenomena to penetrate, and it is at the root of human deception, ignorance, and evil. The important point is, that this poem in the *Songs of Experience* is illustrated with the picture of a man encompassed with a rope (Fig. 75), shown in the same way as in the Arlington Court picture.

The four figures which compose this writhing group (Fig. 55) are in the toils of the evil and illusion which grow from what Blake calls

[1] Keynes edition, page 151. For the male-female and female-male, see also *Milton*, plate 46, lines 17–22; *Jerusalem*, plate 75 (and illustration there), also plate 89, lines 52–62. The horns refer to the Zodiacal sign of Capricorn (the Goat), not Aries (the Ram). For a study of Astrological equivalents in Blake, see E. S. Hamblen, *On the Minor Prophecies of William Blake* (J. M. Dent, 1930), especially chap. 10, 'The Structural plan of the Ancient Wisdom'.

[2] I do not think there is any phallic significance here, as has been suggested.

Abstraction and Mystery. He has devoted several passages to this, both in *Milton* and in *Jerusalem*.[1] He refers to it as:

An Abstract objecting power, that Negatives everything.

It is in this that Satan himself, and the Abomination of Desolation, lie hidden.[2] Caught in these toils of Abstraction, clinging to this rope of self-projected and self-energized Mystery, these writhing human forms will be lead down and down, to where a *black water accumulates*:[3]

The River rises above his banks to wash the Woof:
He takes it in his arms; he passes it in strength thro' his current;
The veil of human miseries is woven over the Ocean.[4]

The cutting of the rope (see Fig. 55) is achieved solely by means of the act of redemption proceeding above on the sea-shore. This cutting symbol in Blake corresponds with his ideas of *A Last Judgment* (not THE Last Judgment, note well). By A Last Judgment Blake meant: *Throwing off Error and Knaves from our company continually and Receiving Truth or Wise Men into our Company continually. . . . Whenever any Individual Rejects Error and Embraces Truth, a Last Judgment passes upon that Individual.*[5] But, says Blake, one cannot be free of evil and error by a mere act of will; there must be A Last Judgment, that is to say, a moment of revealing insight. *Error, or Creation will be burned up, and then, and not till then, Truth or Eternity will appear. It is Burnt up the moment men cease to behold it.*[6] Blake's idea, as stated here, is far subtler and profounder than might be supposed. It is, in fact, not an idea, but something which can be experienced; it can never be defined or described in words. The cutting image, like the Last Judgment image, is an equivalent which indicates the experience which is sought. Both these imply that it is as though seeing Eternity, the Real, and recognizing the relativity of the phenomenal, cuts its binding power.

[1] Blake is particularly explicit about this in *Jerusalem*, plate 10, lines 7–16. In *A Vision of the Last Judgment* (Keynes edition, p. 154) he says in an important passage: 'General Knowledge is Remote Knowledge; it is in particulars that Wisdom consists, and Happiness too.'

[2] See *Milton*, plate 43, lines 43–49.

[3] *Jerusalem*, plate 4, line 10.

[4] *Milton*, plate 31, lines 60–63.

[5] For both sentences, see *A Vision of the Last Judgment* (Keynes edition, p. 156).

[6] Ibid., p. 62.

But Blake very seldom introduced the image of 'cutting' into his designs. The sort of paring and cutting which is attempted in all forms of self-discipline and asceticism, whose aim is to attain some preconceived ideal, this is anathema to Blake. It is therefore necessary to distinguish carefully between these two forms of cutting.

Blake's affirmation that, *Everything that lives is holy*[1] was deeply experienced by him and never contradicted. There is only one thing that may be cut off, and that is Negation, Abstraction, that which does not really live at all, but is a form of self-projected illusion, a parasitic phantasy:

> *All that can be annihilated must be annihilated . . .*
> *There is a Negation, and there is a Contrary:*
> *The Negation must be destroyed to redeem the Contraries.*
> *The Negation is the Spectre.*

These lines come from a very important page in *Milton*; the illustration which accompanies the text shows the act of slaying the many-headed dragon which lurks in the cave in the forest. It is the dragon of Negation, Abstraction, the parasitic demon which threatens human life.[2] But Blake is always careful to distinguish between Negation, in this sense, and the opposites or Contraries, which must always endure and are the very stuff of life. Heresy, false religions, evil in its many forms, may after all be merely manifestations of an over-weighted opposite, or contrary state, as Blake suggests in the prologue to Book 4 of *Jerusalem*, which is addressed to The Christians:

> *Devils are False Religions*
> *'Saul, Saul, Why persecutest thou me?'*

To cut off such manifestations is to cut off the root of the religious impulse itself.

The weavers and spinners on the hillside, from which the flames are issuing, remain to be considered. Here is depicted the work of

[1] The concluding lines of 'A Song of Liberty'.
[2] *Milton*, plate 46, lines 28–37. British Museum copy, plate 42.

Los and Enitharmon—Los labouring at his forge, Enitharmon at her looms and spindles—a theme which runs as a refrain throughout all Blake's major Prophetic Books. Los, with his intuitive imagination, works at his furnaces, melting down the ores and metals, recasting them, and shaping them at his forge. The flames playing around the hill show that Los is at work within.[1] Enitharmon and her daughters ply the looms and spinning-wheels, preparing the threads of fate and the garments for the *Spectrous Souls of the Dead*.[2] What does this signify? It means that the experience of day-to-day existence, which is the material of life, can be shaped and woven in a creative way; it is this day-to-day experience which is the means to the amending of life.

Here is a typical passage on this theme from *Milton*:

Loud sounds the Hammer of Los, loud turn the Wheels of Enitharmon:
Her Looms vibrate with soft affections, weaving the Web of Life
Out from the ashes of the Dead; Los lifts his iron Ladles
With molten ore: he heaves his iron cliffs in his rattling chains
From Hyde Park to the Alms Houses of Mile-end and old Bow.[3]

This is the work that goes on amidst the humdrum round of daily existence. This is the meaning of the furnace and loom symbols in Blake: they refer to the process of day-to-day living, what actually happens, quite apart from the fine theories, philosophies, and ideals. For in this way alone is revealed man's detailed relations with the events, people, and ideas which make up life; and this way leads from particulars to generals. This works in the opposite way to Abstraction, and this experience of the *minute-particulars* of life, if lived through with sensibility and awareness, works against the Spectre:

Within labouring, beholding Without, from Particulars to Generals
Subduing his Spectre, they Builded the Looms of Generation
They builded Great Golgonooza Times on Times, Ages on Ages.[4]

[1] See, for instance, *Jerusalem*, plate 6, where Los is shown at his forge and an aspect of his labour is described; see also plate 8, lines 15–20; plate 10, lines 17–28, &c.

[2] See *Jerusalem*, plate 59, lines 26 to end, and the illustration:

> 'Hour after hour labouring at the whirling Wheel,
> Many Wheels, and as many lovely Daughters sit weeping . . .
> Other Daughters Weave on the Cushion and Pillow network fine. . . .'

[3] *Milton*, plate 6, lines 27–31.

[4] Ibid., plate 3, lines 37–39.

But life is not automatically creative, and although Los and Enitharmon are at work, so too are Rahab and Tirzah. They work in the contrary sense to Enitharmon and her daughters, entangling the skein of fate and enmeshing man ever more and more in the miasma of his efforts and memories:

. . . Tirzah and her Sisters
Weave the black Woof of Death upon Entuthon Benython,
In the Vale of Surrey where Horeb terminates in Rephaim.
The stamping feet of Zelophehad's Daughters are cover'd with Human gore
Upon the treddles of the Loom: they sing to the winged shuttle.
The River rises above his banks to wash the Woof. . . .[1]

Yet this negative fate does not necessarily appear horrific; it may equally appear in the form of enticement, and savour of the subtle spells of enchantment and bewitchment:

Spinning it from their bowels with songs of amorous delight
And melting cadences that lure the Sleepers of Beulah down
The River Storge (which is Arnon) into the Dead Sea.[2]

The river, the weavers and spinners, the hill in flames with Los labouring at his furnaces within—all this is the image of life in the human balance, the life of everyday experience, which holds within itself the crisis of each individual's fate. It is the sifting process which for better or worse must go on to the end of time:

Men understand not the distress and the labour and sorrow
That in the Interior Worlds is carried on in fear and trembling,
Weaving the shuddering fears and loves of Albion's Families.[3]

For this is the place of the *passage through Eternal Death*. But it is only a passage, or way, for the 'awakened' man. Blake represented this awakening in the sixth picture of *The Gates of Paradise* (Fig. 8), which shows a child bursting out of an egg. The state of experience

[1] *Milton*, plate 31, lines 51–63.
[2] Ibid., plate 38, lines 24–31.
[3] *Jerusalem*, plate 59, lines 50–53.

is the passage through Eternal Death and it is a creative process, but only in a negative sense. For it is a becoming aware of, and gaining an insight into, the illusion of the 'created' world of man, which in reality is a cloud of unknowing between him and the eternal. Blake's symbol for this creative process of unknowing is the *City of Golgonooza*. The understanding of illusion, error, the relative, is a negative process which leads back to the starting-point, that is to the state before the Fall; so in this sense it can be regarded as creative. Blake freely used the image of the Fall, and it is clear that it meant to him, not sin, but the difference between the conflicts and strife of illusion, and the integration and harmony of enlightenment:

> *His fall into Division and his Resurrection to Unity:*
> *His fall into the Generation of decay and death, and his*
> *Regeneration by the Resurrection from the dead.*[1]

The state of experience is man's conscious endeavour to find the solution to the conflicts and contradictions of his own human nature. The symbols and images used with reference to this state of experience, and a possible solution, are always paradoxical and contain a seeming contradiction between affirmation and negation: death and life, the grave or tomb and resurrection, generation and regeneration. Blake's point of view, which is so essential to the understanding of his thought, is finely expressed in plate 35 of *Milton*, which is relevant both to the Arlington Court picture, and to *The Gates of Paradise*:

> *Thus they converse with the Dead, watching round the Couch of Death;*
> *For God himself enters Death's Door always with those that enter*
> *And lays down in the Grave with them, in Visions of Eternity,*
> *Till they awake and see Jesus and the Linen Clothes lying*
> *That the Females have Woven for them, and the Gates of their Father's House.*[2]

[1] *The Four Zoas*, book 1, lines 18–20.
[2] *Milton*, plate 35, lines 39–43.

'They' here refers to the *Seven Eyes of God*, which represents a wheel of knowledge possible to human apprehension. The *linen clothes* are the creative aspect of negative thought, the penetration of the cloud of unknowing, of illusion; these clothes can finally be completely discarded. The *Gates of their Father's House* is the apprehension of Divine Union.

Therefore it may be said that the right side of the Arlington Court picture opens up the whole extended commentary of Blake's Prophetic writings on the psychological and spiritual mysteries of life and its processes. Its terms of reference lead on and on into the labyrinth of images displayed in his art. But this, like any other work of Blake's, is only seen rightly when it also leads directly to the simplest realization of the particular problem. It is a statement complete in itself, with clear and vivid meaning, even though the terms of reference contained in it may be seen expanding on all sides.

There is one final figure in the picture to be referred to: the young girl holding the circular skein, who is reclining under a tree near the centre of the picture (Figs. 54 and 57). She seems, to some extent, to link the two sides of the picture; she balances the Vala figure on the sea, and her face shares the radiance of Jerusalem at whose feet she reclines. Like the redeemed form of Ololon in *Milton*, she appears to be a young girl about twelve years old. The meaning of this figure seems to be suggested in the couplets which introduce the prologue of the fourth and last book of *Jerusalem*:

I give you the end of a golden string,
Only wind it into a ball:
It will lead you in at Heaven's gate,
Built in Jerusalem's wall.

If this is indeed her meaning, it resolves the problem, in these terms, into distinguishing between this golden thread and the rope of Abstraction and Negation. But how is it possible to tell the one from the other? The answer must be that the only place where the rope and the net can never thrive is precisely on this threshold of the shore, between heaven and the wild sea. This brings us back to the central image of the picture. Commentary and elucidation have led from image to symbolic image in a maze of words. But within the picture itself is the latent seed of insight, which by means of images goes beyond images: this must remain everyone's own secret. It is the one and only serious function of art to sow this seed.

III

ON THE UNDERSTANDING OF BLAKE'S ART

'IMAGES OF WONDER'

WITH a work of art, the essential thing is to experience it. To experience is not the same thing as to understand. It is one thing to enter into the imaginative world of one of Blake's pictures, his poems, or his myths and to feel the images with their strange and unaccountable vistas awakening within. But it is quite another thing to give a satisfactory account of this experience in terms of the understanding. There is much that may be experienced in one of the simplest of Blake's ineffable poems, or pictures, that overflows any attempt to interpret it. For there is always something implied in the work of art which is beyond thought; something lit up for a moment by the imagination, which is beyond words. If we allow ourselves to enter fully into the experience of a work of art, letting go our rational understanding for the moment, we can become immediately aware of this ineffable quality with its expanding life. This is what Blake invites us to do: *If the Spectator could Enter into these Images in his Imagination . . . or could make a Friend and Companion of one of these Images of wonder . . . then would he arise from his Grave . . . then he would be happy.*[1]

But to experience is not the same thing as to understand. Understanding implies a mental formulation, an interpretation according to conceptual knowledge, and it is just in this that it is important to proceed slowly, and with great reservation. It is all too easy to translate art, which contains the unknown hidden in the incipient hint or implication, into familiar patterns of thoughts, or terms of

[1] Notes on *A Vision of the Last Judgment*; Keynes edition, vol. iii, pp. 153–4.

cognition. But in so doing we lose much of what is important in the work of art. To reduce the unknown forthwith into terms of the known is the temptation which must always be resisted in relation to a work of art. It is as unintelligent as to deny that art has any real and immanent meaning which challenges elucidation. With Blake's art, which is concerned with an unusually subtle calibre of experience, it is especially important to enter fully into its imaginative flight. Only later must come the assimilative processes of understanding. But to experience, in this sense, means to be deeply stirred; and this (although it is the fundamental purpose of art) is what many people instinctively avoid.

As a man William Blake was a seer and devotee intent on studying life in all its fullness and mystery, and in his art he laboured to express this without translating the unknown into terms of the known. His art expresses the living experience in terms of images and symbols. By this means the potential of meaning is retained in dynamic terms of life and energy. His myths and symbolic figures and personages are intent with implicit meaning, which is not reduced to the familiar word, or concept, or formula; he avoided the labels of conventional knowledge and left his images and symbols undetermined, but still in contact with the flux of life. So Blake's art can open our eyes, and shock us into relationship with the living experience. Out of this experience, when gradually and intelligently assimilated, can grow understanding. But it will be a different sort of understanding, not that of conventional, second-hand knowledge, or of the accepted textbooks. It will be understanding which has gone beyond itself, knows its limitations, and knows that it is but a pale reflection of the reality which transcends it.

What faculty enables us to grasp a work of art as a meaningful whole, so that we are moved by it and share its experience as our own? For this surely is the excitement and joy of art, that it expands and fulfils what we already know, or have a taste of, in little. How do we penetrate to the heart of the poem or picture?—a poem such as, *I laid me down upon a bank*, *Where love lay sleeping*, or *Hear the voice of the Bard*, or *Ah, sunflower weary of time*; or a picture such as 'Urizen-Creator', or the Arlington Court picture? The microcosm of meaning each contains is not reached by analysis, or discursive and comparative thinking. These only lead endlessly round the periphery of the artistic microcosm. All that this form of understanding can give, although it may later greatly enrich the meaning, has first to await the spark that will ignite the image at its centre. The power which gives access to the centre and enlightens the work of art with meaning is the intuitive imagination; there is no other means. It is the artist in each of us who alone can understand a work of art. We all have some experience of this artist in ourselves, however immature and undeveloped our intuitive faculty may be. The images and symbols of art are the means of expression of this faculty, and are there to be explored and experienced; just as we must learn about the imaginative experiences of our own lives, our dreams, phantasies, visions, or spiritual experiences.

It is true that sometimes the experience conveyed in art is quite superficial and concerned only with the personal and the accidental. But this is not so with Blake. His art is entirely devoted to psychological and spiritual ends and it constitutes a vast treasure-house of potential life waiting to reveal itself to anyone who cares to look. For this, no initial study or learning is needed, but the spark of intuitive imagination must be there. If it is buried deep, unrecognized, neglected, as happens all too often in our civilization, where conceptual thinking has been developed to the great neglect of the feeling and intuitive faculties, then Blake will certainly appear obscure, difficult, and unaccountable, as will much else in life besides. But if the artist in us is still alive, there will be free response to the vitality hidden in the different levels of Blake's work.

None the less it must be admitted that there is much in Blake which appears confused and turbid. There is the apparent extravagance and exaggeration of many of his pictures, such as, for example, 'Newton', 'Nebuchadnezzar', the 'Good & Evil Angels'. Others, which illustrate Old and New Testament subjects, greatly overstep the forms of accepted iconography as well as the literal context of the Bible itself. The names of the mythical personages of the Prophetic

Books, like the events they undergo and the symbolic names and places with which they are associated, are largely unintelligible to reason and entail a great deal which is apparently arbitrary, contradictory, and inconsistent. The designs which accompany the Prophetic writings rarely seem to illustrate the text literally, and their association with it is often obscure and controversial. Although there may be vivid moments in the Prophetic Books, and passages of moving and intelligible beauty, these only seem to stand out against a background which is turbid, confused, and highly irrational. Indeed, the first impressions of Blake are often like a disturbing dream—a dream of compelling intensity, which lingers in the mind to haunt the memory with its emotions. There is a disquieting feeling of immanent, but hidden meaning, joined with the obscure recollection of some important insight or admonition; but above all there is the baffling sense of incomprehensibility, which flouts all effort at more exact understanding.

If Blake as poet and painter often appears in this way at first encounter, it is not surprising. For Blake was a highly intuitive person and his art is expressed in the intuitive language of images and symbols. To those not familiar with this method of expression and communication, there is much that is disconcerting both in his painting and writing. Whilst drawn towards him and responsive in certain ways, we are none the less exasperated on many counts.

It is very important to realize that there is a great part of life which can only be apprehended by means of images and symbols. It is just that part of life which Western civilization has tended to forget. It is in images and symbols that dreams, phantasies, and visions express themselves; not only those that are trivial, arbitrary, unimportant, but also the deeply significant. Symbols and images are the media of all great and original art, just as they are of all religious and spiritual experiences. For instance, it is this means of expression which is used in the parables of the New Testament. From time immemorial this language of the intuitive imagination has been used by poets, artists, and seers, and has left its traces in the myths, rituals, and religious and artistic documents of mankind. For this is the only means open to man for apprehending the living reality of experience which lies beyond the narrow confines of conventional thinking and knowing. So long as a man is content to live in the petty world of accepted and conventional thought, all appears tidy, logical, comprehensible. But the moment he steps outside this, the moment a bigger and more fundamental experience forces itself upon him, then he is in the world which is only knowable through images and symbols. This is the hallmark of all deep and revolutionary artistic and religious experience. For the symbol or image holds that which transcends the opposite sides of man's nature; it contains that which cannot be filtered into any one part or function of man without overflowing it. The symbol expresses implicitly what cannot be known explicitly. But by means of the symbol it is possible to experience that which cannot be completely understood, for all the diverse elements of man's complicated nature can play their part in it, and have communion with it.

Because Blake is communicating a real and living experience which goes beyond the means of expression of conventional knowledge, his art appears turbid, unaccountable, and to a certain extent unintelligible. This happens with all great innovators in art and religion: 'That is very great. Quite mad. It makes one afraid the house is going to tumble down'—so the aged Goethe commented on listening to the first movement of Beethoven's Fifth Symphony, played to him by Mendelssohn on the piano.[1] After several generations, what appeared titanic and mad, becomes the accepted pattern of thought and feeling of the day. But then the life has already begun to go out of it.

No one has been so influential in showing the importance of the symbol as C. G. Jung. His work has also established a link between dynamic psychology, based on the experimental and scientific approach, and religious psychology. His therapeutic work on neurosis, whose manifestations are so symptomatic of Western man's maladjustment to the world in which he lives, socially, psychologically, and spiritually, has lead Jung to the study of the

[1] Emil Ludwig, *Beethoven* (Hutchinson's International Authors, Ltd., 1944), p. 175.

more esoteric of the great religions and practical philosophies, Eastern as well as Western. For the one can be understood in the terms of the other, to a great extent at least. Jung has thus built a bridge connecting the great intellectual achievements of Western man with the faculties of spiritual and intuitive insight, which are no less precious and indispensible a possession, and still undervalued today.

Jung has been at pains to explain the irrational, but none the less vital, meaning contained in the utterances of symbol- and image-language. In *The Integration of the Personality*, after giving an account of a series of dreams and phantasies, some of which are expressed in pictures, he writes as follows:

'I admit that all this must sound very strange to a reader who is not accustomed to the peculiar language of intuitive processes. They are not directed to the rational mind, which in other ways is man's most valuable achievement. They are spontaneous, dynamic, and bewilderingly devious; they interfuse rational viewpoints with intuitive visions, and ethical values with emotional outbursts. The psychic activity involved in such a process is utterly undifferentiated; it is like a flow of lava in which all sorts of minerals gush forth in one glowing stream, welling up from the entrails of the earth. There is no use in rationalizing and intellectualizing this activity.'[1]

It is hardly necessary to point out that much of this quotation might be a description of Blake's work. Jung concludes by saying that a balance with the rational mind has none the less to be maintained.

Although the sort of experiences described by Jung is largely known to modern psychology as a result of neurosis, and these experiences are therefore forced on individuals in their desperate efforts to achieve adjustment, a larger degree of integration, and so to recover balance, yet it is equally true that such experiences have always been part and parcel of the religious and artistic life. Many motives or causes may lead to a man overstepping, or bursting

[1] C. G. Jung, *The Integration of the Personality* (Kegan Paul, French, Trubner & Co., 1940), p. 42.

through the conventional world, to which his ego-personality is attuned. 'The wind bloweth where it listeth, and thou hearest the sound thereof, but canst not tell whence it cometh, nor whither it goeth: so is everyone that is born of the spirit.'[1] This is the fundamental religious experience, which opens the doors into a reality of far vaster dimensions than that which is locked up and controlled by the ego-personality. 'Is God a Spirit who must be worshipped in Spirit and in Truth, and are not the Gifts of the Spirit Everything to Man?'[2] Yet it is a world not entered without danger, and the relationship with the thinking ego has by some means to be maintained.

The need for this sort of experience has always been regarded as vital in religious psychology and has been taught by all the great spiritual leaders. Jung has studied this in his commentary on an important Chinese text, 'The Secret of the Golden Flower'. He writes:

'What then did these people do in order to achieve the progress that freed them? As far as I could see they did nothing (*wu wei*, inaction) but let things happen, for, as Master Lü Tzŭ teaches in our text, the Light circulates according to its own law, if one does not give up one's accustomed calling. The art of letting things happen, action in non-action, letting go of oneself, as taught by Master Eckhart, became a key to me with which I was able to open the door to the "Way". The key is this: we must be able to let things happen in the psyche. For us, this becomes a real art of which few people know anything. Consciousness is forever interfering, helping, correcting, and negating, and never leaving the simple growth of the psychic processes in peace. It would be a simple enough thing to do, if only simplicity were not the most difficult of all things.'[3]

This idea of letting things happen in the psyche is a very important clue to the understanding of Blake. These inner expressions of the psyche are apt to be so strange, unaccountable, and disturbing that there is usually a strong resistance to them; these psychic

[1] John iii. 8.

[2] *Jerusalem*, plate 77, introduction to chap. 4.

[3] *The Secret of the Golden Flower*, translated and explained by Richard Wilhelm, with a European Commentary by C. G. Jung (Kegan Paul, French, Trubner & Co., 1945), p. 90.

happenings are quickly dismissed or suppressed. Or, rushing to the other extreme, which is equally an evasion of the real issue, phantasies are manipulated and worked up in an artificial way, in the manner of so much contemporary art. Indeed, 'for us, this becomes a real art of which few people know anything'. But Blake was a great master of this art. He understood well the narrow path which must be trod, and perhaps it was partly with reference to this that he wrote on the title-page of the second book of *Milton* (in reversed writing): *How wide the Gulf and Unpassable! between Simplicity and Insipidity.*

In *The Marriage of Heaven & Hell*, Blake expressed some clear views on the subject under discussion. This book was written about the year 1790, when he was still a young man aged thirty-three, and it was the prelude to the tremendous florescence of his illuminated Prophetic Books which thenceforth occupied him till near the end of his life. *The Marriage of Heaven & Hell* is a relatively straightforward and intelligible document and it has always been the most widely read and quoted of his writing, other than his lyrical poetry. It is an important introduction to his views and methods.

In this book he criticizes and shows the limitations of mental distinctions, which divide life into the opposite categories that he labels heaven and hell. Each category has its own standard and principles, which it regards as exclusively valid, and views the other with hostility. Heaven is the realm of the thinking, intellectual mind, with its logic, its order, and its ethical judgements. Hell is the realm of the instincts and emotions, with their impulses, desires, and dynamic energies. The latter, to the mind of rationalistic, Protestant England of Blake's day, appeared as hell, in perpetual enmity with heaven. But Blake's point of view in *The Marriage* is that the one is as essential and real as the other. Heaven and hell, with all that they imply, are relative distinctions which spring from the dualistic mind. Their relativity must never be forgotten, for in fact the one is continually turning into the other, according to the laws of enantiodromia.[1] Although Blake did not use this particular word, he

[1] C. G. Jung, *Psychological Types* (1923), p. 541, &c.; see also *The Integration of the Personality*, p. 121; *Modern Man in Search of a Soul* (1933), p. 275.

referred to this principle in the Fourth Memorable Fancy, where he relates a typical change of one thing into its opposite (see p. 47 above). Moreover, the *Nebuchadnezzar* design, which comes at the end of *The Marriage*, is the pictorial expression of this same principle of enantiodromia, as typified in the Biblical story of Nebuchadnezzar. Blake, throughout, is urging the view, that the living experience, reality itself, is always beyond the opposites, though both are contained in it.

Can Wisdom be put in a silver rod
Or Love in a golden bowl?[1]

Because the rationalistic attitude had obtained such a hold on the European mind of his day, Blake made his protest in *The Marriage.* The prologue, which begins, *Rintrah roars and shakes his fires in the burden'd air*, expresses this protest: because of this contemporary identification of man with the heaven of the mind and its righteousness, Blake found himself in the wilderness *where lions roar*, the place of prophets and of artists who see the need of the time for liberation from the restrictions imposed by the absolute sway of the rational faculties. Hell must be opened up for man to regain his equilibrium. Blake, moreover, tried to show that it is possible to speak in parables, in the symbolic language of images. In this way one can avoid thinking in terms of the opposites; hence the 'Memorable Fancies', or parables (not allegories) of *The Marriage.* He concluded the book with a myth of great significance, which he called a *Song of Liberty*. This short myth, or poem (only twenty verses, with short chorus) expresses Blake's basic experience. But it is expressed exclusively in the language of intuitive imagination, just as the 'Nebuchadnezzar' design is: it means everything, or nothing, according to the person who reads, or sees it.

PSYCHOLOGY OF VISIONS

Blake's art was sadly misunderstood in his own lifetime; it had little meaning and less value for all but a handful of his contem-

[1] Motto to *The Book of Thel.*

poraries. But do we yet understand it rightly? Is sufficient attention paid to the psychological content not only of his writings but also of the designs, which were equally part of his prophetic work? Is there not still a tendency to look too much for aesthetic, formal qualities in his graphic art, in the manner of the aesthetic tradition with which we are so familiar, just as for long the romantic overtones of his poetry tended to obscure their religious, occult, and meditative character? I would like here to suggest that the intent and purport of his art—his graphic art just as much as his prophetic writings—is primarily contemplative, in the sense that word is used in religious practice, and it is just this which is insufficiently appreciated. Later I will point to some parallels between his ideas about the imaginative faculty, and his exercise of it, and certain theories and methods of meditation known to Eastern religious thought. But here I want to begin by emphasizing the noetic quality of the images and symbols by means of which he expresses himself; for it is only in relation to the psychological, or religious aim of his work, that they can be rightly understood.

The whole intent of Blake's art is spiritual, if we understand rightly what that means. Blake's spiritual effort was not concerned with the propagation of any particular Faith or dogma, nor with the effort to approximate life and conduct to any *a priori* pattern, ideal, or moral code. His efforts were devoted to finding Truth, or reality, in the experience and understanding of life, which involves the whole man at work in the crucible of the life-experience. Seeing the truth, or reality, and becoming one with it, entails the experiencer and that which is experienced. In so far as the experiencer is limited, conditioned, malfunctioning, so will the experience be partial, biased, and deranged. The need for the unitive experience is paramount, as Blake always insists, but the experiencer has so isolated and malformed himself that direct contact with that which transcends the personal and the individual is no longer easy and natural for him. The intuitive imagination is the means to this expanding and unitive vision.

If the Spectator could Enter into these Images in his Imagination, approaching them on the Fiery Chariot of his Contemplative Thought . . . then would he arise from his Grave, then would he meet the Lord in the Air. . . .' As a faculty the intuition is a link with that which transcends the individual; but in itself it is more than this, for it can lead to, and indeed become, participation in the unitive experience of reality itself: *the Human Imagination which is the Divine Vision and Fruition, in which Man liveth Eternally.*[1] Or again: the *Imagination, the real and eternal world.*[2] But a man is kept back from this, his vision is obscured, he is isolated and confined, because of his illusory attachments and his inner conflicts. The experiencer has to be reconditioned, reintegrated, if he is to have anything more than fleeting and haphazard glimpses of that which is not only vaster and more dynamic than he is, but also immeasurably more refined.

Blake's art, therefore, emphasizes that the supersensual experience is always accessible to man and that it is in fact his inheritance by his very nature: *the Divine Vision remains Everywhere, Forever.*[3] But he is equally intent on showing why, and in what ways man has broken himself off from it, and how he is consequently unhappy and tormented in himself. *If the doors of perception were cleansed everything would appear . . . as it is, infinite.*[4] But these doors are not cleansed. Far from it, man is in a state of psychological chaos and disorder; one psychological function struggles against another; he is divided between competing centres of desire, with their rival wills and censorships; he dare not let go of himself, lest his inharmonious nature with its fierce impulses should immediately show itself. Sometimes it does, and man is swept away in mass movements by the tremendous psychic forces which he has not learnt to know and integrate. Then takes place the rush of the Gadarene swine, as in Blake's day with the French Revolution, or on an even bigger scale in our own day; the real tragedy being that most of the vast masses involved do not realize they are acting in a demoniac way, whilst the others who are aware of the catastrophe do not see what can be

[1] For the first quotation, see *Milton*, plate 35, lines 19–20; for the second, see p. 111 note 1.
[2] *Jerusalem*, plate 77; prologue to chap. 4.
[3] *Milton*, plate 24, line 2.
[4] *The Marriage of Heaven and Hell*; Keynes edition, p. 189.

done to prevent such subhuman disasters. Without harmony, how can there be clarity? So Blake is much concerned with holding up the mirror to this distorted state of man. Only by cleansing his senses can man come to the infinite; and with man as he is, there is a long way to go.

This is Blake's great task in the Prophetic Books. In *The Four Zoas* he recounts how individual man has denied the Divine Vision, cut himself off from the unitive state, and therefore fallen into division, that is, into the state of 'generation' and death. He is then at war within himself and his psychological functions, instead of working in harmony, are in perpetual conflict, whilst all effort only seems to lead farther towards disintegration and struggle. The whole immense poem is a representation of this, studded with intimations of the integrated, unitive state. The positive and negative aspects of vision are in continual interplay. *Milton* again describes the fall and consequent state of conflict, first from the point of view of Blake's own personal problems as an artist in the service of his patron Hayley during his three years stay at Felpham; secondly relative to the poet Milton, who typifies the problems of the artist struggling with the particular aberrations of his cultural environment. The Spectre of Albion, *Who made himself a God and destroyed the Human Form Divine*,[1] represents the root error of the civilization in which Blake lived. His intent, here as always, was to reveal this error, and so re-establish the way. *Jerusalem* begins with the two lines:

> *Of the Sleep of Ulro! and of the passage through*
> *Eternal Death! and of the awakening to Eternal Life.*

Blake's art was equally directed to an exposition of these three states. First the state of sleep, or subhuman existence, cut off from the Divine Vision and ignorant of it. Second, to stirring man to the struggle with experience, to the exploration of relative knowledge, and the integration of his individuality. Thirdly, to the going beyond all this and the opening up of *the Eternal Worlds*.[2]

In studying Blake it is very important to realize that vision, or

[1] *Milton*, plate 35, line 13.

[2] *Jerusalem*, plate 5, line 18.

the intuitive imagination, has two complementary aspects, which from a superficial point of view often appear contrary to one another. Intuitive imagination reveals the Divine Vision, but it also reveals man's limitations and all the distortions of his fallen and divided nature. Man being in the parlous state he is, vision for him is largely a question of seeing his aberrations reflected against the stainless mirror of the real. It therefore appears largely a negative admonitory thing. This negative aspect of vision, as I shall call it, plays a large part in Blake's work and we shall have to go into it further. What is essential to realize is that it is an integral part of vision in the fullest sense.

Blake says: *Vision or Imagination is a Representation of what Eternally Exists, Really and Unchangeably. Fable or Allegory is Form'd by the daughters of Memory. Imagination is surrounded by the daughters of Inspiration, who in the aggregate are call'd Jerusalem.*[1] Here he is stressing first and foremost the unitive aspect of the intuitive imagination. In this it is in complete contrast to other forms of cognition, which involve thought processes based on memory. But in the third sentence quoted, he alludes to the mirror-like activity of intuition, which makes it a revealing link between the different sides of man's nature. This is its negative, admonitory aspect. For although the doors of our senses are defiled, and the experiencer is still badly out of tune with the real, yet he has this intuitive faculty which links him with the truth, and at the same time acts like a mirror, revealing his imperfections and his defilements. Blake emphasizes this in a passage which he wrote for the prologue to the first chapter of *Jerusalem*:

The Spirit of Jesus is the continual forgiveness of Sin: he who waits to be righteous before he enters into the Saviour's kingdom, the Divine Body, will never enter there. I am perhaps the most sinful of men. I pretend not to holiness: yet I pretend to love, to see, to converse with daily, as man with man, and the more to have an interest in the Friend of Sinners.

Since these two aspects of vision, the unitive and the negative

[1] Notes on *A Vision of the Last Judgment*; Keynes edition, p. 145.

aspect, are always in close relationship one with another, Blake's art in the main is a process of negative exposition. His revelation and analysis of psychological and spiritual sickness is apt to disturb some of his readers. They feel his writing and his art is concerned unnecessarily with the negative, deranged, fearful, and horrifying aspects of man's life. But when this relationship between the positive and negative aspect of the intuitive processes is appreciated, Blake's work will be found to be inspired with a fine sense of harmony. A much finer relationship is maintained between this positive and negative, than by all but a very few of our modern psychologists, who so rarely have a positive, spiritual alternative to put beside their necessarily negative analysis.

Nevertheless, Blake's art in the main is a negative process of knowledge and insight. It expresses that which is awry with the psyche; life itself will know how to mend and re-create, once the diseased and erroneous is thrown out. This is the method of all true spiritual work, no matter the name of the religion or discipline according to which a man may be working; for spiritual knowledge always consists in negatives. The positive spiritual insight, or experience, so far transcends knowledge that it is always, and completely, unknowable. The author of the *Cloud of Unknowing* quotes St. Denis: 'The most goodly knowing of God is that, the which is known by unknowing.' Krishnamurti says, with his unrivalled directness and simplicity: 'Is not the highest form of thinking the completely negative state of the mind in which there is no accumulation, in which therefore there is complete poverty of mind—poverty in the most dignified, profound sense? It is new soil, it is a mind in which there is no knowledge; therefore it is the Unknown.' Or, in Blake's own words:

To cleanse the Face of my Spirit by Self-examination
To bathe in the Waters of Life, to wash off the Not Human.[1]

The positive aspect of the intuitive imagination links man with the

[1] *The Cloud of Unknowing*, edited by Evelyn Underhill (John M. Watkins, 1946), p. 189. *Krishnamurti's Talks in India* (Poona and Bombay), 1953 (Krishnamurti Writings Inc.), p. 91. *Milton*, plate 47, line 37 to plate 48, line 1.

infinite; it is his essential capacity to be one with *the Eternal Great Humanity Divine.*[1] The negative aspect reveals how far the individual is out of alignment with his essential nature. In this sense it works in a corrective and compensatory manner and clarifies distinctions between the personal and the supra-personal, the sensual and the super-sensual. It distinguishes the psychological complex from the psychological principles which underlie it. It reveals the great archetypal principles and images—the *eternal attributes*[2] as Blake calls them—clarifying for the individual his relationship with them; by contrast it throws into relief the egocentric whims and inclinations of his more personal existence. It is the means by which man can judge himself and weigh the significance of his experience and his psychological values:

> *Judge then of thy Own Self: thy Eternal Lineaments explore,*
> *What is Eternal and what Changeable, and what Annihilable.*[3]

This same idea is put in a different way and elaborated in another passage:

What is Above is Within, for everything in Eternity is translucent;
The Circumference is Within: Without, is formed the Selfish Center;
And the Circumference still expands going forward to Eternity,
And the Center has Eternal States! these States we now explore.[4]

Further, these two aspects of vision, the positive and the negative, can be thought of from the point of view of the relation between time and eternity, the phenomenal and the absolute. Man contains within himself the seed of eternity, and yet he lives in the phenomenal world of time. Until he recognizes these dual roots of his nature and the need to harmonize them, his struggles and problems only mount upon him. Blake was always drawing attention to this. Pointing to the fact that phenomenal existence is the finite expression of the absolute, he says: *Eternity is in love with the productions of time.* In the same sense he speaks of *Jesus, the image of the Invisible God*;

[1] *Milton*, plate 2, line 8.
[2] *A Descriptive Catalogue*; Keynes edition, vol. iii, p. 101.
[3] *Milton*, plate 35, lines 30–31.
[4] *Jerusalem*, plate 71, lines 6–9.

and he asserted to Crabb Robinson that every man is a more or less limited and imperfect expression of the divine.[1] He therefore uses the word Jesus (complimentary to Albion, or human nature) exactly in the way Buddha, or Buddha-nature, is used in Mahayana Buddhism. But the opposite aspect of the temporal and phenomenal is alluded to when he says: *Time is the mercy of Eternity; without Time's swiftness . . . all were eternal torment.*[2] For time is the medium in which attainment to the infinite is possible. Time and eternity, the phenomenal and absolute, are contingent and man has the means and possibility of stepping from one to the other.

The essence of Blake's art is, therefore, the relation of these two, the temporal and the eternal, and the means of this relationship is the intuitive imagination which shows the nature of both. Vision is a way of seeing by means of images and symbols. It is direct apprehension of psychic events, of 'what is' (to use Krishnamurti's phrase) in regard to subjective experience. Blake says: *A Spirit and a Vision are not, as the modern philosophy supposes, a cloudy vapour or a nothing: they are organised and minutely articulated beyond all that the mortal and perishing nature can produce. . . . The painter of this work asserts that all his imaginations appear to him infinitely more perfect and more minutely organised than anything seen by his mortal eye.*[3] But what are these spirits and visions, and how can these images of reality be perceived? This is the 'real art of which few people know anything'. It is the art of inner vision and contemplation, which allows things to happen in the psyche and brings about action through non-action.

What is revealed in this way is of the greatest possible importance. Blake writes about it as follows:

Visions of these eternal principles or characters of human life appear to poets, in all ages; the Grecian gods were the ancient Cherubim of Phoenicia; but the Greeks, and since them the Moderns, have neglected to subdue the gods of Priam. These gods are visions of the eternal attributes, or divine names, which, when erected into gods, become destructive to humanity.

[1] *The Marriage of Heaven and Hell* (aphorisms); Keynes edition, p. 184; *Milton*, plate 2, line 12; for Henry Crabb Robinson's Diary, see Arthur Symons, *William Blake* (Constable, 1902), part ii.

[2] *Milton*, plate 26, lines 72–73.

[3] *A Descriptive Catalogue*; Keynes edition, p. 108.

They ought to be the servants and not the masters of man, or of society. They ought to be made to sacrifice to Man, and not man compelled to sacrifice to them; for when separated from man or humanity, who is Jesus the Saviour, the vine of eternity, they are thieves and rebels: they are destroyers.[1] These 'eternal attributes', or 'divine names', are archetypal principles which dominate and transcend man's personal life.[2] The individual's relation to these 'dominants of the unconscious', these supra-personal psychic energies, is of the greatest importance. If they are not seen and recognized, and so to some extent assimilated with consciousness, they control man entirely from the unconscious. So long as man fails to understand these psychic forces, they can at any time dominate him and become destructive forces. To erect these archetypes into gods, as is done in popular religions, is not to understand them. This is an intermediary, separative process, which by no means is a solution; it leads to the oppression of the individual by the gods of the day, be they cult images, moral codes, or rationalized social virtues. Because, although separated from the individual and projected in the form of religious or social creeds, their energy still remains an unconscious force. It is only by the assimilative process of understanding that they can be subjected to man, that is to mankind as a whole and not the individual. Otherwise they must always remain potentially destructive forces, like the evil spirits unleashed into the Gadarene swine.[3]

This, then, is the task of the truly spiritual man and the real Christian. It is the task Blake set himself in his prodigious artistic

[1] *A Descriptive Catalogue*; Keynes edition, p. 101. Compare with this passage, plate 11 of *The Marriage of Heaven and Hell* (Fitzwilliam Museum, Riches copy); Keynes edition, p. 187.

[2] Compare the following pronouncement of Blake on archetypal images: 'The Nature of Visionary Fancy, or Imagination, is very little known, and the Eternal nature and permanence of its Ever Existant Images is considered as less permanent than the things of Vegetative and Generative Nature; yet the Oak dies as well as the Lettuce, but its Eternal Image and Individuality never dies, but renews by its seed; just so the Imaginative Image returns by the seed of Contemplative Thought . . .' (Notes on *A Vision of the Last Judgment*, Keynes edition, p. 146).

[3] See C. G. Jung, *Essays on Contemporary Events* (Kegan Paul, 1947), especially 'Wotan', pp. 12–13. Also 'Epilogue', pp. 75–76: 'When archetypes appear in a collective form we have to meet the great danger of a mass-movement. A catastrophe can only be avoided by the presence of a majority of individuals who understand something of the effect of an archetype and can thus intercept it. At the very least there must be a certain number of such individuals whose influence can still make itself felt.'

activity; for unless the few 'just men' capable of this work can be found, Sodom and Gomorrah will surely be destroyed in each succeeding age. *I know of no other Christianity and of no other Gospel than the liberty both of body and mind to exercise the Divine Arts of Imagination: Imagination, the real and eternal World of which this Vegetable Universe is but a faint shadow. . . .*[1] This affirmation of Blake's is therefore no mere pious idea, as is all too commonly supposed. It is an exercise requiring the greatest possible energy and skill, an art of which few indeed are capable. For humanity it is a task of the greatest possible significance.

When in *Milton* Blake writes: *Within labouring, beholding Without, from Particulars to Generals Subduing his Spectre . . .*[2] the emphasis given to inner work refers precisely to this. The work has to take place within, where the psyche can speak and act. That which is without, which has already been projected, can only be beheld, or observed. Once outside it can no longer be radically altered. The work which frees, and integrates, and regenerates, can only be accomplished within. It is this inner work, the art at which Blake was such a master, that is so little understood or studied. As Jung has said: 'We Westerners, in spite of our so-called culture, are still barbarians and children when it comes to the psychic world.'[3]

ART, RELIGION, AND MEDITATION

Art and religion have often worked together in close alliance, but the idea of art as a means to spiritual enlightenment has become quite foreign to European thought since the Middle Ages. A. K. Coomaraswamy, in his book *The Transformation of Nature in Art*, has written about the theory underlying the practice of art in India, which he maintains is in accord with a universal point of view. 'It does not in fact differ from what is implicit in the Far Eastern view of art, or on the other hand in any essentials from the Scholastic Christian point of view, or what is asserted in the aphorisms of

[1] *Jerusalem*, plate 77, prologue to chap. 4.
[2] *Milton*, plate 3, lines 37–43.
[3] *The Integration of the Personality*, p. 41.

Blake; it does differ essentially from the modern non-intellectual interpretations of art as sensation.'[1]

Coomaraswamy has made a very interesting study of Meister Eckhart's view of art, in a chapter in this same book, and he has pointed out that 'Eckhart's nearest and natural descendant is Blake'.[2] He derives Eckhart's ideas about art principally from his Sermons, which 'might well be termed an Upanishad of Europe'. Describing these ideas he writes:

'The work of art, man's "creature", is by the same token, even more than by its substantial distinction from the object, conventional; to be interpreted and understood not as a direct reflection of the world as the world is in itself, but as a symbol or group of symbols having an ascertained rational significance and even deeper content, not functioning only as means to recognition but as means to communication and to vision. Thus with reference to the interpretation of scripture and myths in general, and the same holds good for any other kind of art, "the material things in themselves, they say, must be translated to a higher plane. . . . All the stories taken from them have another esoteric meaning. Our understanding of them is as totally unlike the thing as it is in itself and as it is in God, as though it did not exist", but there is more in the work of art than can be understood, "none so wise as but when he tries to fathom them will find they are beyond his depth and discover more therein." Art is simultaneously denotation, connotation, and suggestion; statement, implication, and content; literal, allegorical, and anagogic.'[3]

In this passage Coomaraswamy is quoting chiefly from Sermon CII, where Eckhart also says: 'The teaching of our school is that anything known or born is an image.'[4]

Meister Eckhart's attitude, although close to medieval Christian Scholasticism, is a far remove from Protestant thought, says

[1] A. K. Coomaraswamy, *The Transformation of Nature in Art* (Harvard University Press, 1934), p. 56.

[2] Ibid., p. 202 (note 57).

[3] Ibid., pp. 83–84.

[4] *Meister Eckhard*, by Franz Pfeifer, translated by C. de B. Evans (John M. Watkins, 1947), vol. i, p. 258.

Coomaraswamy: 'The real analogy between Eckhart's modes of thought and those which have long been current in India should make it easy for the Vedantist or Mahayana Buddhist to understand him, which would require a much greater effort on the part of a Protestant Christian or modern philosopher.' He continues: 'Eckhart's whole conception of human life in operation and attainment is aesthetic. . . . Art is religion, religion art, not related, but the same.'[1] This, of course, is essentially Blake's point of view and Coomaraswamy refers to a number of Blake's aphorisms, for instance:

> *'Jesus and his [apostles and] Disciples were all Artists.'*
> *'Praise is the Practice of Art.'*
> *'In Eternity All is Vision.'*[2]

It will be of interest in the understanding of Blake's art to know something about the ways in which art is practised and used in India, according to the traditions of Vedanta and Yoga, as a means towards spiritual insight and realization. But first it is important to emphasize that Blake's views about vision, and the imagination, are by no means peculiar to Blake, or an idiosyncrasy of his. His point of view corresponds with that of Eckhart. It also finds classic expression in the form of a theory and teaching about the intuitive imagination, in the Lankavatara Sutra, which is one of the central documents of Mahayana Buddhism. The following quotations from the Lankavatara Sutra will, I believe, throw much light on Blake's ideas as outlined in the previous section. In the Sutra three forms of mind are postulated, Universal Mind, discriminating mind, and an intuitive mind, the latter entering into the two others and forming a link between them.

'Universal Mind is like a great ocean, its surface ruffled by waves and surges, but its depths remaining forever unmoved. . . .'

'The discriminating-mind is the cause of the sense-minds and is their support and with them is kept functioning as it describes and becomes attached to a world of objects, and then, by means of its

[1] A. K. Coomaraswamy, op. cit., pp. 61–62.

[2] Ibid., p. 202 (note 57).

habit-energy, it defiles the face of Universal Mind. Thus Universal Mind becomes the storage and clearing house of all the accumulated products of mentation and action since beginningless time.

'Between Universal Mind and the individual discriminating-mind is the intuitive-mind which is dependent upon Universal Mind for its cause and support and enters into relations with both. It partakes of the universality of Universal Mind, shares its purity, and like it, is above form and momentariness. It is through the intuitive mind that the good non-outflowings emerge, are manifested and are realised. Fortunate it is that intuition is not momentary, for if the enlightenment which comes by intuition were momentary, the wise would lose their "wiseness" which they do not. But the intuitive-mind enters into relations with the lower mind system, shares its experiences and reflects upon its activities. . . .

'The discriminating-mind is a dancer and a magician with the objective world as his stage. Intuitive-mind is the wise jester who travels with the magician and reflects upon his emptiness and transiency. Universal Mind keeps the record and knows what must be and what may be. . . .[1]

'. . . intuitive-mind . . . is the link between the intellectual-mind and Universal Mind. While it is not an individualized organ like the intellectual-mind, it has that which is much better—direct dependence on Universal Mind. While intuition does not give information which can be analysed and discriminated, it gives that which is far superior—self-realization through identification.'[2] These and other passages in the Lankavatara Sutra should be studied by anyone interested in Blake's views on the imagination, and his descriptions of the manifestations of Los and Enitharmon, their relationships with the other Zoas, and with Urthona.

Let us now return to the theme of art as a medium of spiritual enlightenment. The best and most complete study of Indian art

[1] The Lankavatara Sutra, quoted from Dwight Goddard, *A Buddhist Bible* (1938), pp. 306–7. Parts of this are quoted by Oswald Siren, *The Chinese on the Art of Painting* (1936), pp. 98–99.

[2] The Lankavatara Sutra, op. cit., pp. 315–16.

from this point of view is, so far as I know, Heinrich Zimmer's *Kunstform und Yoga im Indischen Kultbild.*[1] This book is a study of the principles and forms of art in relation to the religious ideas and methods of the Vedanta. Zimmer has based his study largely on the Tantric texts and their commentaries, since the Tantra is the interpretation of Vedanta for the present epoch. Yoga, according to its various schools, is the practice of these theoretical ideas.

Zimmer explains that art, in the form of the cult-image, is regarded as one of the essential means to religious experience which is available to man, and it has been extensively made use of in the various schools and cults which spring from Vedanta. Man is a fraction of the Absolute; but finding himself living and struggling in the phenomenal world of time, he seeks to reunite himself with the Absolute by awakening the Atman, which is contained in essence within him. Realization of the Atman, whose essence is one with the Absolute, is his aim. This is the central idea of the Vedanta, and in its pursuit certain forms of meditation are practised which include the use of Yantras, Mantras, and cult-images (Pratima). A Yantra is a symbol in the form of a diagram, or purely linear image (circle, triangle, &c), and the word Yantra is used as the basic concept for the symbol-image. A Mantra is its verbal form, and Pratima is the cult-image which combines aesthetic and feeling contents with the pure symbol (Yantra).

Following Zimmer, let us briefly consider the theory underlying the use of a Yantra in meditation. According to Vedanta and its literary expression in the Tantra, the Absolute is unknowable and undifferentiated; and yet man is not utterly without relationship with the Absolute. This is represented by the concept, or rather symbol, of Shiva-Shakti, the dual aspect of God is so far as He is knowable. Shiva, the male form, is the undifferentiated Absolute. Shakti, the female, represents the expression of the Absolute in time, God's creation, and his power. As Shakti, the Absolute manifests in the world known to man, descending through the ever-coarsening levels of Maya. In this process of creation, the clear light of the

[1] Published by Frankfurter Verlags-Austalt, Berlin, 1926.

Absolute is split and fractured and becomes the impure world of phenomenal existence. The Tantra shows the way back to purity and unity by means of the use of images. For duality is the nature of consciousness, and yet reality is non-dual. Consciousness must therefore find the means to transform itself. The seer and the seen, the experiencer and the experience, must again achieve unity; this miracle of transformation must be found in the transcendental experience of samadhi. The Yantra is an instrument for this.

A Yantra is a diagram or symbol, by means of which the real, or that which approximates more closely to the real, can be apprehended by the inner vision. It is an aspect of reality on a higher level, which is difficult to attain to from the lower and refractory levels of Maya. As already said, the Yantra in its pure form is a linear diagram, such as, for example, the Shri Yantra (nine triangles plotted in a certain relation with a circle). A Mantra is regarded as a special type of Yantra; it is a word formula, or symbol contained in verbal form (*Om Mani Padme Hum*). Pratima is a cult-image or work of art; it is a special type of Yantra into which feeling and sensation enter to a much greater degree than in the pure Yantra. Obviously, from the point of view outlined here, it is just these feelings and sensations which are relatively of the least importance. Whilst they serve to link man's phenomenal nature with his higher nature, it is what he sees with the inner eye of vision that is of real importance. This inner image is recognized as something essentially archetypal, or supra-personal. The whole effort in the use of the cult-image, or work of art, is directed towards this realization, or insight. The apprehension of a higher aspect of reality, of unitive vision, is the aim.

The Vedanta teaches that there is no reality in the external form of the image. The image, or work of art in itself, is meaningless except as a means to an end; that end is the attainment of an inner experience. Now the inner world of psychological, or spiritual energy and activity is always projecting itself on to the outer world of man's experience. For a man to understand the world in which he lives, his relationship with it, and what he himself is expressing outwardly in his life, he must become familiar with his own psychological projections. He must learn to see them, discriminate them, and become familiar with them. By means of meditation he can enter into relation with them, and watch them, as it were in play. One of these forms of meditation, which can be described as active phantasy, is concerned with the seeing of symbols and diagrams, which can afterwards be drawn or painted. Yantras are often drawn on paper or sand, and then thrown away or rubbed out. Images (Pratima) are also modelled in clay; these too are usually thrown away.[1] For none of these things are important in themselves: they are only a means to an end. Even this practice of meditation itself, once the more perfect forms of Samadhi are attained, is discontinued, at least according to Vedanta theory.

Zimmer gives a short account of a form of meditation employing symbols and images which are of considerable interest in relation with Blake's work; the following quotation is an extract from this:

'These preliminary exercises should fill him (the initiate) with the certainty that he is ready to experience the Revelation of Truth, which will unfold within him in the form of dynamic and fluid images. To conclude these exercises he now pronounces the great formulae which are expressed in the Mandala known as: The Wisdom of the other Shore: "Om, I am clean (*shuddha*) in my essence, as all things are clean (empty) in their essences"—and: "my essence is the Diamond of the Knowledge of Emptiness."

'In these formulae he anticipates in thought processes what he will experience in himself in visions.

'Out of the emptiness which is his own essence, he develops a picture of the whole world; this is analogous to the apparent manifestation of the pure Godhead in the phenomenal. What he experiences is nothing else but his own Being in his various spheres of material and spiritual existence, and it will therefore take on the form of the embracing couple Mahâsukha and his Beloved.

[1] One is reminded of the following anecdote related by Crabb Robinson: 'He will not print any more. "I write", he says, "when commanded by the spirits and the moment I have written I see the words flie about the room in all directions. It is then published and the spirits can read. My MSS. [are] of no further use. . . .' Blake was a puzzle to Crabb Robinson; but it seems more than likely that he had been speaking about the principle of meditation referred to here. See Arthur Symons, op. cit., Part II, p. 268.

'In accordance with the traditional Brahmin teaching of the Creation, he next lets that which is unformed and nameless (which he knows to be the emptiness which is his own essence) change itself into the four elements, which issue one from the other. Out of emptiness proceeds air, out of air fire, out of fire water, and finally out of water earth. Whilst he lets this process develop he brings the symbols of the four elements before his inner eye. The symbols are: a white semi-circle with waving banners, a red triangle with a flaming jewel, a white circle with a vessel, and a yellow square with a triangular thunderbolt at each corner. They appear from the void and issue from each other, as the mystical syllables (Mantra-Shakti) called them up; for these syllables are their manifestations in the realm of sound. The syllable "yam" is air and produces its equivalent symbolic image; "ram" is fire, "vam" is water and "lam" is earth. They develop out of the inner image of the syllables, just as out of the syllable "sum" rises the shining apparition of the Divine Mount Sumeru, the axis of the world-egg, whose jewel body has four sides, which are composed of crystal, gold, ruby and emerald. They sparkle with the colours of the four quarters of the world. A practising Hindu would see on the summit the Palaces of Indra, King of the Gods and his Blessed ones: Amarâvatî "Abode of the Immortals". In its place, an adept versed in the Buddhist Mandala develops the vision of the Temple of a monastery (*Vihâra*) as the only place worthy of the Buddha: a square building made of jewels, with four doors—one on each side—surrounded by magic walls of diamond (*vajra*). Its roof rises to a cupola, like the stupas on earth, which contain reliquaries and bear witness to the attainment of Nirvâna by the Enlightened Ones. Its very centre is formed by a circle and the eight petals of a lotus flower. They point to all the directions of the compass (the four quarters and their intermediary points). On the lotus the disciple sees his own self in the form of Mahâsukha embracing the female body. As the "Supreme Bliss of the Circles" (*cakramahâ-sukha*) he sees himself with four heads and eight arms, and by means of contemplation realises the essence of his Being. His four heads signify the four elements, earth, water, fire, and air in their immaterial, supra-sensual condition; but at the same time they are also the four infinite emotions (*apramâna*). The absorption of these images into himself helps him to progress nearer towards Nirvana. The four infinite emotions are: infinite compassion (*karunâ*), infinite love (*maitrî*), infinite serenity (*muditâ*) and infinite calm (*upekshâ*). Further they signify the four forms of knowledge; that is knowledge of the emptiness of Being as well as non-Being (*bhâva* and *abhâvashûnyatâ*), of the emptiness of Essence (*paramârthashûnyatâ*) and the complete equality of all things in their essential Emptiness. The face in front is blue, the reverse red; the faces to the right and left are green and yellow; thus they rule the quarters of the world. Each face has three eyes, which see the past, present and future; they confront all three worlds: the world of the senses (*kâmaloka*), the multiform world of supra-sensual vision (*rûpaloka*), and the world empty of forms belonging to the highest attainment of Yoga (*arûpaloka*)'.[1]

This somewhat theoretical reconstruction of a form of meditation, which necessarily leaves out all that is tenuous and spontaneous, is none the less relevant to Blake's art; there is even a definite analogy between the symbols used and the meanings attached to them. Indeed, a study of Eastern forms of meditation, whether Vedantist or Mahayana Buddhist, makes it clear how much they have in common with Blake's visions expressed in his Prophetic Books. The imaginative use of images, the transmutation processes, the noetic intent, all this is the same.[2] The fact is that the symbols of art, used for spiritual ends, are analogous with those used in other forms of meditation, and are developed from the faculties of inner vision. Whilst these images and symbols constitute a power of apprehending reality, they must obey its laws and to this end alone must they strive to be true.

[1] H. Zimmer, *Kunstform und Yoga im Indischen Kultbild* (Berlin 1926) pp. 77–79. Author's translation.

[2] In this connexion, it is worth referring to the commentary written by C. G. Jung on the Sutra of Meditation on Amitayus (Amitaynr-Dhyana-Sutra), which is a Sanscrit Yoga text of the fifth century B.C., known from a Chinese translation. See C. G. Jung, 'On the Psychology of Eastern Meditation', in *Art and Thought* issued in honour of A. K. Coomaraswamy, edited by K. Bharatha Ilyer, pp. 169–79.

Blake always emphasizes the reality of vision and that which the intuitive imagination reveals: *The Eternal Body of Man is the Imagination,* he says, and again: *Vision or Imagination is a Representation of what Eternally Exists, Really and Unchangeably.* Once this is truly realized, as he points out in *The Gates of Paradise,* then a real beginning can be made with life, as distinct from Sleep (Ulro), and Experience (Death):

> *But when once I did descry*
> *The Immortal Man that cannot Die*
> *Thro evening shades I haste away*
> *To close the Labours of my Day.*

The intuitive imagination reveals '*eternal principles*', '*visions of the eternal attributes or divine names*'. Such statements by Blake are equivalent to the Vedanta view referred to above which underlies the use of the Yantra in its various forms.

It has already been noted that there is much in Blake's art which is archetypal in nature, and of universal validity, although this is not always immediately apparent. His myths, images, symbolic names, and personages can be compared with the archetypal symbols studied in Jungian psychology; also with the figures of the Bible, Kabala, and many branches of Mythology. But to trace these parallels with a view to establishing influences and derivations, rather than to amplify their meaning, is to mistake the point. It is to confuse the finger pointing at the moon with the moon itself. Blake's aim was to see reality, and through experience of it to come to union with it. To understand Blake we must know this and share in the spirit of his work. When he uses phrases, incidents, and stories taken from the Bible or the Kabala, it is to amplify and elucidate his context. He uses these traditional symbols much as the Vedantist might use a Yantra or Mantra for the purposes of meditation; a traditional formula is taken as a point of reference. But in themselves neither Mantra nor Bible text have any value or meaning until the reality from which they issued has been re-experienced. Except as a means to an end, and that the reawakening of insight and inner awareness, all these remain mere lifeless things. If quoted for the sake of authority or erudition, or as a mask for uncertainty, they constitute a hindrance rather than a help. Blake is probably seldom guilty of this misuse of the traditional symbol, this meaningless repetition and copying of the dead letter of the outward form. If he is guilty of it, as many lesser poets and mystics have been, it is the duty of the commentator to point this out. But he must not think that tracing the sources of Blake's images in any way explains them, or that parallel citations are of any particular interest in themselves. Blake's realization, that is the noetic content which he is trying to express, is alone valid and important.

Some of the archetypal symbols reenunciated by Blake in his own terms have already been pointed out, in the two former chapters. In these Blake realized anew the equivalent of a perennial manifestation of an aspect of reality. Such symbols are: (1) the male and female, or light and dark principles, representing the creative and receptive, the formative and the conditioned aspects of life; equivalents are the Yang-Yin of Taoism, the Shiva-Shakti of the Vedanta; (2) Albion, the Great Man, equivalent to Adam Kadmon of the Kabbala, and to Narāyana, the Cosmic Man of Indian mythology; closely related with The Eternal Great Humanity Divine, equivalent to the Christian Jesus, and to Buddha, or Buddha-nature of Mahayana Buddhism; (3) Fourfold man, expressed by the Four Zoas, equivalent with the living Creatures of the Apocalypse, the four psychological functions of Jungian psychology, the fourfold division experienced in certain Eastern meditations (cited above), the four fixed signs of the Zodiac, &c.; (4) the feminine figure representing the unconscious in its many different aspects, particularly as Vala—Jerusalem, equivalent to the dark and light anima of Jungian psychology; (5) Orc (the 'generate Luvah'), the fierce figure of aggression, which psychoanalysis finds playing such a prominent part in man's unconscious; (6) the construction of the Arlington Court picture according to the principle of the circle and the quaternity, with emphasis on the numbers three and four, as found in the

Mandalas of Tantric Buddhism, Boehme's 'Philosophic Globe', the Shri Yantra of Vedanta (circle and nine triangles), and the enneagram of Raymond Lully (circle with ninefold division).[1]

The above list is arbitrary and brief and is intended merely to refer to a few symbols which have been given prominence in the course of the commentaries undertaken in this book. But it is sufficient to show how Blake is far less arbitrary and extravagant in his symbols than might superficially be supposed. The same can be said about his 'right and left' symbolism. This is also archetypal, as can be experienced (and habitually is) by anyone for himself in his dreams and phantasies. But because it is archetypal it does not mean that it can be elevated into a law or formula. Rather, it is something which has to be recognized, and understood according to the significance of the context.

Blake's adherence to the truth of the inner image, and his devotion to the paramount importance of the intuitive realization, is clearly shown in the oscillation of his art between two contrary standpoints, the aesthetic and the ontological. For whilst some of Blake's designs can be regarded as purely aesthetic, in the modern Western sense, others are decidedly ontological or didactic in character. For instance, his pictures of 'The Last Judgment', 'The Laocoon', or 'The Gates of Paradise', are much less aesthetic than didactic; their ontological character is very much in evidence. In fact, Blake's art is never entirely aesthetic, although often mistaken as such; nor is it ever entirely ontological. It swings between these two poles and always contains elements of both. The reason for this can readily be understood in the light of what has been said about the Vedanta theory of the Yantra.

Since Blake's concern is for the noetic quality of the intuitive vision, he employs the means best suited to grasp this in each particular case, both in his writing and in his art. If the aesthetic development of an image will prove the most revealing, then his art has a strongly aesthetic flavour. Likewise, if the description of an event or situation is better apprehended through a strong appeal to

[1] Ramon Lull, *Ars Inventiva Veritatis* (Valencia, D. de Gumiel, 1515).

the feelings, then his verse is rich in poetical tones. In these contexts the noetic quality of the images often remains unsuspected, or is only very superficially explored, as with the 'Nebuchadnezzar' and the 'Good and Evil Angel' colour-prints, or the 'Temptation of Eve' tempera. But in these, and similar examples, Blake has not really been carried away with an access of extravagant emotion (or 'enthusiasm' as his contemporaries called it). Nor are his illustrations of Bible stories by any means as vapid and pious as might readily be supposed. He is using his art to suggest, to hint at spiritual states, or principles, of which he himself had some direct experience.

On the other hand, his art is sometimes Spartan in its aesthetic bearing. It can be pared down to the starkest lineaments of image and phrase. Witness, for instance, *The Gates of Paradise*, whose text reads like a series of abstract formulas, and whose pictographs share some of the coldness of diagrams; here, the noetic, ontological aspect of his work is in the ascendant. So also with *The Laocoon*, his drawing of a cast of the Graeco-Roman statue, which he has covered with texts, quotations, and aphorisms, referring to the symbolic ideas the statue awakened to Blake's inner vision. In the *Illustrations of the Book of Job*, the aesthetic and ontological elements are more evenly balanced, and this probably accounts for the better understanding of this work and the recognition it has always received. But what are we to think of the pictures of *The Last Judgment* and *The Fall*? Looking at the Petworth or Victoria and Albert Museum pictures they might well be mistaken for illustrations of the apocalyptic accounts in the Bible. In a sense, it is true, they are that; but how deeply so, and how much more besides, is only apparent when one reads his notes on *A Vision of the Last Judgment*, which happen to have survived in one of his notebooks. For Blake this was a vision he had actually experienced; he expressed it largely in Bible terms, but his notes show how vivid and original was the meaning for him of the personages and events which constitute these terms.

Attention must now be drawn to one more aspect of Blake's

vision; this is his power to see, or the recorded experience of his having seen, the infinite in everything:

To see a World in a Grain of Sand
And a Heaven in a Wild Flower
Hold Infinity in the palm of your hand
And Eternity in an hour.[1]

Or, as he put into the mouth of the prophet Isaiah, *My senses discovered the infinite in everything.*[2] This was also the experience of Thomas Traherne: 'You never enjoy the world aright, till you see how a sand exhibiteth the wisdom and power of God'; or: 'You never enjoy the world aright, till the Sea itself floweth in your veins, till you are clothed with the heavens, and crowned with the stars: and perceive yourself to be the sole heir of the whole world, and more than so, because men are in it who are everyone sole heir as well as you.'[3]

For not only is the infinite present in everything, but one thing is the mirror of another, and everything is linked and harmonized in a translucent chain of correspondences. This is the translucence of which Blake often speaks. Eckhart said, 'anything known or born is an image', and Jacob Boehme could see the inner life and nature of every natural object recorded on it like a 'signature' (as described in his book *De Signatura Rerum*). In the poem sent to his friend Thomas Butts from Felpham, which begins, *To my Friend Butts I write / My first Vision of Light. . .*, Blake describes the miracle of the divine manifesting in the phenomenal. The poem records an instance of the power of contracting and expanding vision, which is one of Blake's fundamental images, to which allusion has already been made in Chapter I. This contracting and expanding of consciousness is the essence of human life; it is that which makes possible the co-existence in one body of the divine and human. In the *Four Zoas* Blake writes:

Then those in Great Eternity met in the Council of God
As one Man, for contracting their Exalted Senses

[1] 'Auguries of Innocence'.

[2] *The Marriage of Heaven and Hell*; Keynes edition, p. 187.

[3] Thomas Traherne, *Centuries of Meditations*, edited by Bertram Dobell (Dobell, 1950 edition), pp. 18–19.

They behold Multitude, or Expanding they behold as one,
As One Man all the Universal family.[1]

In *Jerusalem* he explains further:

Let the Human Organs be kept in their perfect Integrity
At will Contracting into Worms, or Expanding into Gods,
And then, behold! What are these Ulro Visions of Chastity?
. . . for tho' we sit down within
The plowed furrow, listening to the weeping clods till we
Contract or Expand Space at will: or if we raise ourselves
Upon the chariots of the morning, Contracting or Expanding Time
Every one knows, we are One Family: One Man blessed for ever.[2]

This stanza indicates, by means of images, man's ability to live in the phenomenal world and yet remain in harmony and contact with the absolute:

At will to murmur in the flowers small as the honey bee,
At will to stretch across the heavens and step from star to star.[3]

In studying Blake, it is important to realize that he was a religious man and an imaginative artist; he saw an identity of aim in these two capacities, for he owned to no dogma or revelation other than those of his own insight, his own realization.[4] To be busy with worldly affairs, to be a *slave of the world and time*, he accounted atheism.[5] It is therefore necessary to bear in mind the sort of admonition which is usually found in religious documents; it is well expressed in 'The Great Tantra of Liberation'; 'The highest standpoint is that where the presence of Brahmah is seen in everything. The middle attitude is that of seeing within; the lowest is that of song

[1] *The Four Zoas*, book 1, lines 467–70.

[2] *Jerusalem*, plate 55, lines 36–46.

[3] *The Four Zoas*, book 2, lines 297–8.

[4] For instance: 'Jesus and his Apostles and Disciples were all artists'; 'Christianity is Art and not Money'; the *Laocoon*: 'I know of no other Christianity and of no other Gospel than the liberty both of body and mind to exercise the Divine Arts of imagination . . .'; *Jerusalem*, plate 77 (preface to chap. 4). His unorthodoxy is particularly apparent in 'The Everlasting Gospel'.

[5] See, for instance, Mona Wilson, *The life of William Blake* (London 1948), p. 313, quoting his views on Dante and Wordsworth.

and recitation of words. Lower than the lowest is bare external worship.'[1] The need is emphasized here to assess correctly different kinds of understanding, and different levels of consciousness. We must be careful to judge rightly about Blake's standpoint. It is easy to degrade Blake by reducing his work to an ordinary mundane or political level, but this is to render meaningless that part of it which is of greatest value.

In common with other religious or mystical writers of great originality,[2] Blake declared his purpose at the beginning of his Prophetic Books and indicated the spirit in which they should be read. In the preface to *Milton* he appealed against rationalism (which he equated with the classical tradition) and urged the need for a more inspirational attitude. He appealed against the *Daughters of Memory* to the *Daughters of Inspiration*, then he burst out with the poem *And did those feet in ancient time* . . . which is surely one of the greatest songs of spiritual aspiration in all mystical literature. In *Jerusalem*, his preface *To the Public* (divided as 'Sheep' and 'Goats') is a challenge to understand him rightly. Much of the warning it contains (about the God of Fire?) is unfortunately now erased; but the famous passage about forgiveness of sins and communion with the Divine (already cited, p. 106) leads up to the poem with the lines

> *Again he speaks in thunder and in fire !*
> *Thunder of Thought, and flames of fierce desire:*
> *Even from the depths of Hell his voice I hear*

By means of vision and insight it is his declared purpose to reintegrate hell, earth, and heaven.

Visions and phantasies are the very stuff of human consciousness. They have to be seen, awakened, and then thoroughly experienced and assimilated, if man's spiritual and psychological problems are

[1] H. Zimmer, op. cit., p. 40. Compare Blake: 'The outward Ceremony is Antichrist' (The *Laocoon*).

[2] Three examples are: (1) *The Cloud of Unknowing*, edited by Evelyn Underhill (John M. Watkins, 1946), the Prologue of which contains a serious warning; (2) Jacob Boehme, *The Way to Christ* (John M. Watkins, 1927), the Preface, which also warns as well as instructs; (3) the *Mathnawi* of Jalalu'ddin Rumi (translated by R. A. Nicholson, Cambridge, 1926), Proem to Book I, which suggests the author's standpoint in the subtlest poetry.

ever to be resolved and transcended. Blake was a master at observing these turbulent psychic happenings, these utterances of the unconscious. He respected the equivocable nature of dreams and phantasies, treating them with forbearance and allowing them to play out their drama to the full, for he knew their true value, and that wisdom and understanding could be harvested in this way.

He seems to have deliberately invented new names for his mythological personages and places, and other symbols, for he realized that the very effort to express himself by means of art and poetry was a safeguard against the tame and fruitless business of translating the unknown into terms of the known; because rationalization is the very antithesis of the artistic activity. Whilst he constantly refers to Bible texts, and to Christian and Old Testament symbols and images, his own story with its mythological protagonists always holds the centre of the stage. By this means he keeps the actuality of his inspiration alive, so that it may continually renew itself and develop. It is as though he realized that, if he did not proceed in this bold, intuitional way, every symbol he used, and each experience he tried to express, would immediately be equated with some outworn myth and threadbare idea. All the old labels would be promptly reapplied. Nothing new would be surmised; his work might be more easily accepted, but there would be no burning impact, no crisis of experience, nothing new would be understood. It is in this same experimental, intuitive spirit that we should approach his work.

NOTES

NOTE A, p. 22. For example: *A Vision of the Last Judgment*: 'Albion . . . in whose Sleep, or chaos, Creation began (Keynes edition, p. 152). *Milton*, plate 22, line 25: 'Now Albion's sleeping Humanity began to turn upon his Couch.' *Jerusalem*, plate 15, lines 9–10: 'O Divine Spirit sustain me on thy wings! That I may awake Albion from his long and cold repose.' *Jerusalem*, plate 94, line 1; 'Albion cold lays on his rock'; plate 95, lines 5–6: 'The Breath Divine went forth over the morning hills, Albion rose in anger'; plate 97, lines 6–7: 'Then Albion stretch'd his hand into Infinitude, And took his Bow.' See also p. 65, n. 2 and Note F.

NOTE B, p. 22. Compare this couplet from *The Gates of Paradise* with:

> Can that which was of woman born
> In the absence of the Morn
> When the Soul fell into Sleep
>
> . . . .
>
> Rooting over with thorns and stems
> The buried Soul and all its Gems.

From the *Everlasting Gospel* (d) (Keynes edition, p. 329); this was written about the year 1818.

NOTE C, p. 25. For instance: *Milton*.

> 'Contraries are Positives
> A Negation is not a Contrary' (plate 33 (chapter heading)).
> 'There is a place where Contraries are equally True' (plate 33, line 1).
> 'There is a Negation, and there is a Contrary:
> The Negation must be destroyed to redeem the Contraries (plate 46, lines 32–33).
> 'To where the Contraries of Beulah war beneath Negation's banner' (plate 38, line 23).

NOTE D, p. 26. *The Four Zoas*, book 1, lines 6–10:

> 'Four Mighty Ones are in every Man; a Perfect Unity
> Cannot exist but from the Universal Brotherhood of Eden,
> The Universal Man, To whom be Glory Evermore. Amen.
> What are the Natures of those living Creatures the Heav'nly Father only knoweth. . . .'

W. P. Witcutt has made a very interesting study of the Zoas in relation to

Jungian psychology in his book, *Blake, a psychological study* (Hollis & Carter, 1946). The earlier chapters in this book are brilliant.

NOTE E, p. 61. For Moses see Exod. iii. 2–4. For Swedenborg compare the following passage: 'Flames signify confirmation; such a flame has, by the Divine mercy of God Messiah, appeared to me many times, and indeed of various sizes, and of different colour and lustre; so that while I was writing a certain little book, scarcely a day passed, for several months, without a flame appearing to me as bright as a chimney fire; this was at the Time a sign of approbation, and it was before the Time when spirits began to speak with me in audible voice.' *Adversaria*, vol. iii, no. 7012; quoted by R. L. Tafel, *Documents concerning the life and character of Emanuel Swedenborg*, vol. ii, part 1, p. 145 and note (Swedenborg Society, 1877). See also Swedenborg's *Spiritual Diary* (5 vols., James Speirs, 1902), nos. 2676, 2677 (on 'little Fires and Stars').

Pictorial examples in Blake's work are: 'God clothing Adam and Eve' (water-colour, Fitzwilliam Museum); 'So Los arose' (*Europe*, last plate, 18 in Fitzwilliam Museum, Riches copy); compare *Jerusalem*, plate 95, and plate 6 (Los at his forge). The inscription connected with a sketch for the last plate of *Milton* is significant; it reads: 'Father and Mother, I return from flames of fire tried and pure and white' (see Keynes edition, vol. ii, p. 397, note to plate 50). But it must always be remembered that fire and flames are of different kinds, symbolically; three distinct categories are shown in the Arlington picture.

NOTE F, p. 65. *Jerusalem*, plate 3, prologue to Chap. 1, 'To the Public', line 30. See also plate 4:

> 'Of the Sleep of Ulro! and of the passage through Eternal Death!
> and of the awakening to Eternal Life' (opening lines of chap. 1).
> '. . . thy sister and thy daughters
> Weep at thy soul's disease, and the Divine Vision is darken'd' (lines 12–13).

In *Milton*, plate 17, lines 36–46, Milton sees:

> Albion upon the Rock of Ages
> Deadly pale outstretch'd and snowy cold, storm cover'd.

See also Note A.

NOTE G, p. 80. It would be interesting to construct a set of symbols, in the manner of the trigrams of the *I-Ching*, based on Blake's Four Zoas and their emanations. By postulating eight different states or situations in which these eight Zoas and their emanations are described in Blake's Prophetic Books, the sixty-four situations represented by the hexagrams could be obtained. A commentary could be deduced from Blake's texts. As a method of study this might prove rewarding, and it would certainly bring into evidence Blake's subtle perception of the laws of change and enantiodromia, which is the divine play ('Lila') between the opposites.

SELECT BIBLIOGRAPHY

1. CHRONOLOGICAL LIST OF BLAKE'S ILLUMINATED AND ENGRAVED BOOKS

(*a*) *The Illuminated Books*

(See The Grolier Club of New York, *William Blake, Illuminated Books, A Census*, compiled by G. Keynes and E. Wolf 2nd, 1953, for details and locations of extant copies.)

There is no Natural Religion	*c.* 1788
All Religions are One	*c.* 1788
Songs of Innocence	1789
The Book of Thel	1789
The Marriage of Heaven and Hell and A Song of Liberty	*c.* 1790–3
Visions of the Daughters of Albion	1793
America, a Prophecy	1793
Songs of Innocence and of Experience	1794
Europe, a Prophecy	1794
The (First) Book of Urizen	1794
The Book of Ahania	*c.* 1795
The Book of Los	1795
The Song of Los	1795
The Four Zoas, or Vala (manuscript only)	1795–1804
Milton, a Poem in two Books	1804–8
Jerusalem, The Emanation of the Giant Albion	1804–18
The Ghost of Abel	1822

(*b*) *The Engraved Books*

The Gates of Paradise: for children	1793
The Gates of Paradise: for the sexes	1818
Illustrations of the Book of Job	1825

2. SELECTED FACSIMILES OF THE ILLUMINATED BOOKS

Jerusalem. London (Trianon Press, published for the William Blake Trust), 1952. Heliogravure facsimile printed in black (uncoloured) with additional typographical reprint with numbered lines.

Linnell-Rinder copy.

Jerusalem. London (Trianon Press, published for the William Blake Trust), 1951. In colour.

Stirling, now Yale University Library copy.

The Book of Thel. London (Gollancz); New York, 1928.

British Museum copy.

The Book of Urizen, with notes by Max Plowman. London and Toronto (Dent), 1929.

Dimsdale copy.

The Marriage of Heaven and Hell, with notes by Max Plowman. London and Toronto (Dent), 1927.

Fitzwilliam Museum copy.

The Songs of Innocence. London (Trianon Press, published for the William Blake Trust), 1954.

Rosenwald—Library of Congress copy of *c.* 1790.

The Songs of Innocence and Experience. London (Trianon Press, for the William Blake Trust), 1955.

Rosenwald—Library of Congress copy of 1826.

Visions of the Daughters of Albion, with notes by John Middleton Murry. London and Toronto (Dent), 1932.

British Museum copy.

3. THE TEXT OF THE POETRY AND PROSE (including the Illuminated Books)

GEOFFREY KEYNES, *The Writings of William Blake*, in 3 vols., illustrated. (Nonesuch Press, London, 1925.)

GEOFFREY KEYNES, *William Blake, Poetry and Prose*, in 1 vol. (less strictly chronological than the 3-vol. edition). (Nonesuch Press, London, 1927.)

H. M. MARGOLIOUTH, *William Blake's Vala*, Blake's numbered text. This is a reconstruction of the MS. text of 'Vala' before it was altered into its later form as 'The Four Zoas'. (Oxford, Clarendon Press, 1956.)

4. THE PRINCIPAL PUBLIC COLLECTIONS (containing Blake's drawings, water-colour and tempera paintings, engravings, illuminated and engraved books)

(*a*) *Great Britain*: Arlington Court, Devon (National Trust); Bodleian Library and Ashmolean Museum, Oxford; British Museum, London; City Art Gallery and Museum, Birmingham; Fitzwilliam Museum, Cambridge; City Art Gallery and Museum, and Whitworth Art Gallery, Manchester; National Gallery of Scotland, Edinburgh; Tate Gallery, London; Victoria and Albert Museum, London.

(*b*) *U.S.A.*: Fogg Art Museum, Cambridge, Mass.; Harvard College Library, Cambridge, Mass.; H. E. Huntington Library, San Marino, California; Lessing J. Rosenwald Collection, National Gallery of Art, Washington, D.C.; Library of Congress, Washington, D.C.; Metropolitan Museum, New York City;

Museum of Fine Arts, Boston; New York Public Library, New York City; Pierpont Morgan Library, New York City; Yale University Library, New Haven, Conn.

(*c*) *Australia*: National Gallery of Victoria, Melbourne.

5. BOOKS ILLUSTRATING BLAKE'S GRAPHIC ART

LAURENCE BINYON. *The Drawings and Engravings of William Blake.* 104 plates, of which 16 in colour. London (The Studio), 1922.

LAURENCE BINYON. *The Engraved Designs of William Blake.* 82 plates, several in colour. London, 1926.

The companion volume to Figgis's *Paintings.* Includes a catalogue of all the original designs engraved by Blake.

DARRELL FIGGIS. *The Paintings of William Blake.* 100 plates. London, 1925.

FOGG ART MUSEUM: *Blake's Illustrations for Dante.* Picture Book No. 2. Cambridge, Mass., 1953.

FOGG ART MUSEUM. *Illustrations to Young's Night Thoughts, done in water-colours by William Blake.* 5 coloured, 25 monochrome reproductions. Essay by Geoffrey Keynes. Cambridge, Mass., 1927.

GEOFFREY KEYNES. *Blake Studies—Notes on his life & works.* 48 plates. London, 1949.

GEOFFREY KEYNES. *Blake's Pencil Drawings: Second Series.* 56 plates. London, 1956.

GEOFFREY KEYNES. *Engravings by William Blake: The Separate plates.* 45 plates. Dublin, 1956.

GEOFFREY KEYNES. *Pencil Drawings by William Blake.* 82 plates. London, 1927.

GEOFFREY KEYNES. *The Note-Book* (*Rossetti M.S.*) *of William Blake.* With photographic reproductions and transcriptions. London, 1935.

GEOFFREY KEYNES. *William Blake's Engravings.* Fully illustrated. London, 1950.

H. E. HUNTINGTON LIBRARY. *Catalogue of William Blake's Drawings & Paintings,* by C. H. Collins Baker. 24 plates. San Marino, California, 1938.

LONDON, BURLINGTON FINE ARTS CLUB. *Catalogue of Blake's Centenary Exhibition.* 49 plates. London, 1927.

The illustrations are large and excellent.

LONDON, NATIONAL ART COLLECTIONS FUND. *Illustrations to the Divine Comedy of Dante by William Blake.* 102 plates. London (privately printed), 1922.

Excellent illustrations.

PHILADELPHIA MUSEUM OF ART. *Descriptive Catalogue of an Exhibition of the works of William Blake selected from Collections in the U.S.A.* Fully illustrated. Philadelphia, 1939.

PIERPONT MORGAN LIBRARY. *Illustrations of the Book of Job by William Blake.* Being all the water-colour designs, pencil drawings, and engravings reproduced in facsimile. Introduction by Laurence Binyon and Geoffrey Keynes. In 6 fascicules. New York, 1935.

The definitive work on the subject.

W. GRAHAM ROBERTSON. *The Blake Collection of W. Graham Robertson.* Introduction by Kerrison Preston. 64 plates. London, 1952.

(Published for the William Blake Trust.)

ALBERT S. ROE. *Blake's Illustrations to the Divine Comedy.* 103 plates. Princeton, New Jersey, 1953.

Excellent illustrations.

A. G. B. RUSSELL. *The Engravings of William Blake.* 32 plates. London, 1912.

Includes a catalogue of the engravings of his own designs and of others (but only the separate plates).

The Illustrations of William Blake for Thornton's Virgil, with the First Eclogue and the Imitation by Ambrose Philips. Reproduced together with 8 blocks in their original state, 16 pencil designs and a set of electro-type prints from the wood-blocks. Introduction by Geoffrey Keynes. London, 1937.

JOSEPH H. WICKSTEED. *Blake's Vision of the Book of Job.* Fully illustrated. London, 1910. 2nd ed. London and New York, 1924.

6. STANDARD BIOGRAPHY

The standard biography of Blake at present is:

MONA WILSON. *The Life of William Blake.* New edition. London, 1948.

The first edition was published by the Nonesuch Press, 1927.

ADDENDUM

The Complete Writings of William Blake, edited by Geoffrey Keynes (Variorum edition, in one volume, verse lines numbered), Nonesuch Press, London, 1957.

INDEX OF QUOTATIONS FROM BLAKE

GENERAL INDEX

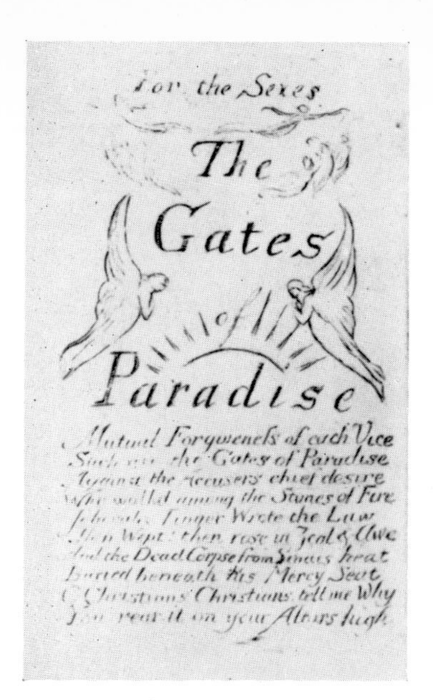

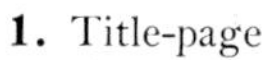

1. Title-page

2. (Frontispiece). 'What is Man!'

3. The Child-Mandrake

THE GATES OF PARADISE

4. Water

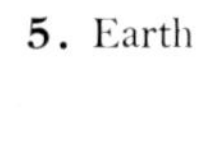

5. Earth

6. Air

7. Fire

THE GATES OF PARADISE

At length for hatching ripe
he breaks the shell
6
Publishd by W Blake 17 May 1793

8. Child hatching from Egg

9. 'Alas! What are these?'

10. 'My Son!'

9
I want! I want!
Pub d by W Blake 17 May 1793

11. Climbing to the Moon

THE GATES OF PARADISE

12. Time's Ocean

13. Aged Ignorance

14. Ugolino

15. Vision

THE GATES OF PARADISE

16. The Traveller hasteth

17. Death's Door

18. The Worm-Mother

19. (Tail-piece). The Spectre

THE GATES OF PARADISE

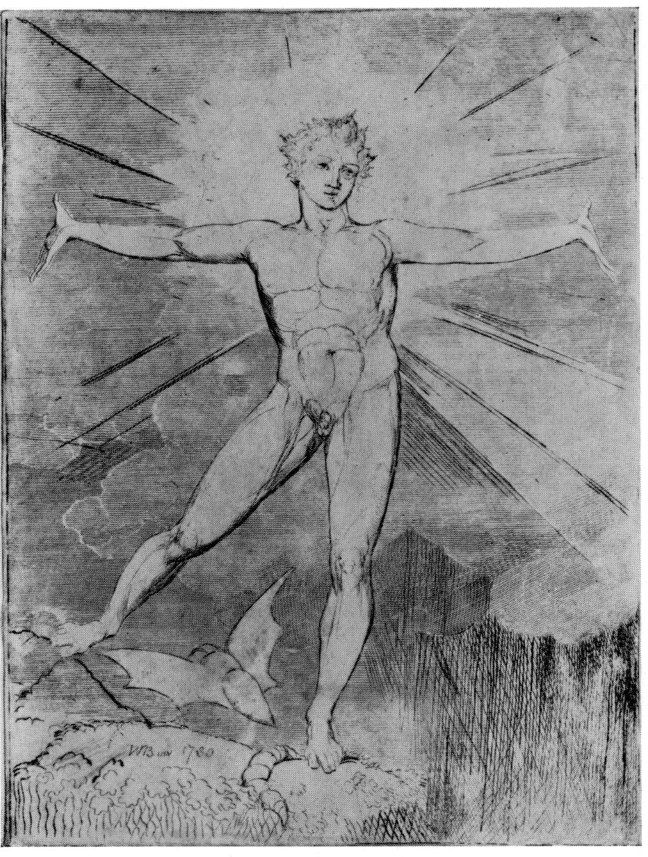

20. Albion Rose, or Glad Day

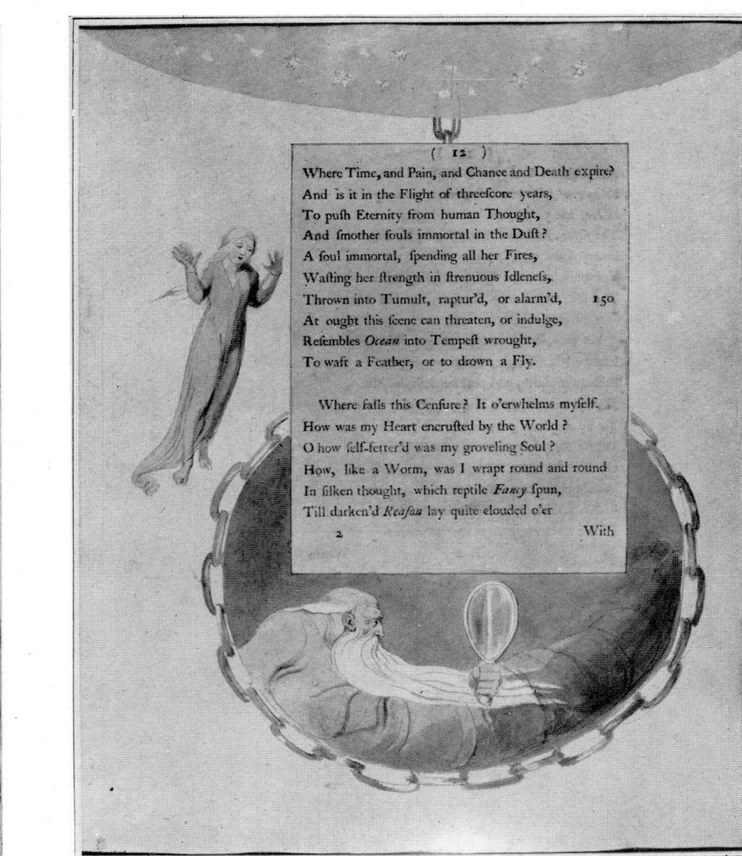

(12)

Where Time, and Pain, and Chance and Death expire?
And is it in the Flight of threeſcore years,
To puſh Eternity from human Thought,
And ſmother ſouls immortal in the Duſt?
A ſoul immortal, ſpending all her Fires,
Waſting her ſtrength in ſtrenuous Idleneſs,
Thrown into Tumult, raptur'd, or alarm'd, 150
At ought this ſcene can threaten, or indulge,
Reſembles *Ocean* into Tempeſt wrought,
To waft a Feather, or to drown a Fly.

Where falls this Cenſure? It o'erwhelms myſelf.
How was my Heart encruſted by the World?
O how ſelf-fetter'd was my groveling Soul?
How, like a Worm, was I wrapt round and round
In ſilken thought, which reptile *Fancy* ſpun,
Till darken'd *Reaſon* lay quite clouded o'er

2 With

21. 'A worm seventy inches long'

22. The Three Accusers

23. The Covering Cherub

The Just Upright Man is laughed to scorn

24. Job accused by his three friends

25. The Self-hood overthrown

The terror answerd: I am Orc, wreath'd round the accursed tree:
The times are ended; shadows pass the morning gins to break;

26. The Stone of Night

Why should Punishment Weave the Veil with Iron Wheels of War
When Forgiveness might it Weave with Wings of Cherubim
Loud groand Albion from mountain to mountain & replied

27. Wings of Cherubim and Iron Wheels of War

28. *Europe* (the title-page)

29. The Temptation of Eve

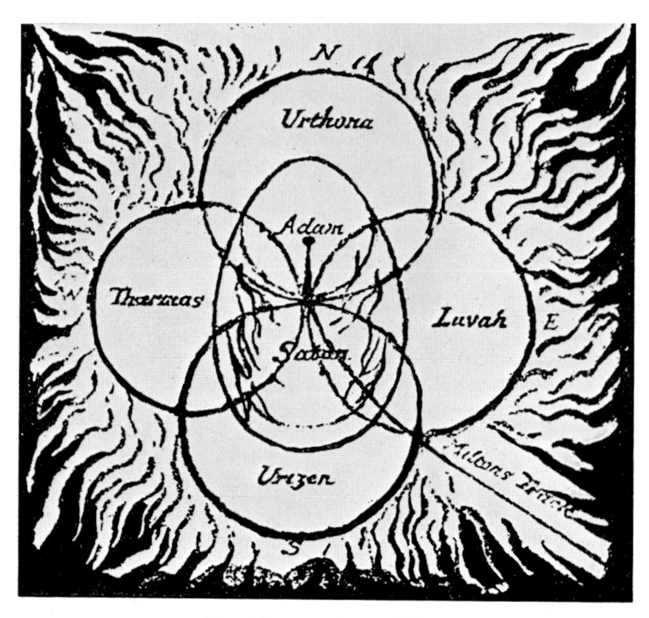

30. Diagram from *Milton*

31. Satan exulting over Eve

And Rahab Babylon the Great hath destroyed Jerusalem
Bath stood upon the Severn with Merlin & Bladud & Arthur
The Cup of Rahab in his hand: her Poisons Twenty-seven-fold
And all her Twenty-seven Heavens now hid & now reveald
Appear in strong delusive light of Time & Space drawn out
In shadowy pomp by the Eternal Prophet created evermore
For Los in Six Thousand Years walks up & down continually
That not one Moment of Time be lost & every revolution
Of Space he makes permanent in Bowlahoola & Cathedron.
And these the names of the Twenty-seven Heavens & their Churches
Adam. Seth. Enos. Cainan. Mahalaleel. Jared. Enoch.
Methuselah. Lamech: these are the Giants mighty, Hermaphroditic
Noah. Shem. Arphaxad. Cainan the Second. Salah. Heber.
Peleg. Reu. Serug. Nahor. Terah: these are the Female Males:
A Male within a Female hid as in an Ark & Curtains.
Abraham. Moses. Solomon. Paul. Constantine. Charlemaine
Luther. these Seven are the Male Females: the Dragon Forms
The Female hid within a Male: thus Rahab is reveald
Mystery Babylon the Great: the Abomination of Desolation
Religion hid in War: a Dragon red & hidden Harlot
But Jesus breaking thro' the Central Zones of Death & Hell
Opens Eternity in Time & Space; triumphant in Mercy
Thus are the Heavens formd by Los within the Mundane Shell
And where Luther ends Adam begins again in Eternal Circle
To awake the Prisoners of Death; to bring Albion again
With Luvah into light eternal, in his eternal day.
But now the Starry Heavens are fled from the mighty limbs of Al-
bion

32. Dragon-females

12
And the clouds & fires pale rolld round in the night of Enitharmon
Round Albions cliffs & Londons walls; still Enitharmon slept:
Rolling volumes of grey mist involve Churches, Palaces, Towers:
For Urizen unclaspd his Book: feeding his soul with pity
The youth of England hid in gloom curse the paind heavens; compelld
Into the deadly night to see the form of Albions Angel
Their parents brought them forth & aged ignorance preaches canting,
On a vast rock, perceivd by those senses that are closd from thought:
Bleak, dark, abrupt, it stands & overshadows London city
They saw his boney feet on the rock, the flesh consumd in flames:
They saw the Serpent temple lifted above, shadowing the Island white:
They heard the voice of Albions Angel howling in flames of Orc,
Seeking the trump of the last doom
Above the rest the howl was heard from Westminster louder & louder:
The Guardian of the secret codes forsook his ancient mansion,
Driven out by the flames of Orc; his furrd robes & false locks
Adhered and grew one with his flesh, and nerves & veins shot thro them
With dismal torment sick hanging upon the wind: he fled
Groveling along Great George Street thro' the Park gate; all the soldiers
Fled from his sight: he dragd his torments to the wilderness.
Thus was the howl thro Europe!
For Orc rejoicd to hear the howling shadows
But Palamabron shot his lightnings trenching down his wide back
And Rintrah hung with all his legions in the nether deep
Enitharmon laughd in her sleep to see (O womans triumph)
Every house a den, every man bound; the shadows are filld
With spectres, and the windows wove over with curses of iron:
Over the doors Thou shalt not; & over the chimneys Fear is written:
With bands of iron round their necks fastend into the walls
The citizens: in leaden gyves the inhabitants of suburbs
Walk heavy: soft and bent are the bones of villagers
Between the clouds of Urizen the flames of Orc roll heavy
Around the limbs of Albions Guardian, his flesh consuming.
Howlings & hissings, shrieks & groans, & voices of despair
Arise around him in the cloudy
Heavens of Albion, Furious

33. The Veil

34. The Elohim creating Adam

35. Los enters Death's Door

Eastward & Southward & Northward are Incircled with flaming fires.
And the North is Breadth. the South is Heighth & Depth:
The East is Inwards: & the West is Outwards every way.
And Los beheld the mild Emanation Jerusalem eastward bending
Her revolutions toward the Starry Wheels in maternal anguish
Like a pale cloud arising from the arms of Beulahs Daughters:
In Entuthon Benythons deep Vales beneath Golgonooza.

36. Los's Vision of Jerusalem

Thy mother lays her length outstretch'd upon the shore beneath.
Sound! sound! my loud war-trumpets & alarm my thirteen Angels!
Loud howls the eternal Wolf! the eternal Lion lashes his tail!

37. The Puer Eternus

38. The Living Moment between the Opposites

His Spectre driv'n by the Starry Wheels of Albions sons, black and
Opake divided from his back; he labours and he mourns!
For as his Emanation divided, his Spectre also divided
In terror of those starry wheels: and the Spectre stood over Los
Howling in pain: a blackning Shadow, blackning dark & opake
Cursing the terrible Los: bitterly cursing him for his friendship
To Albion, suggesting murderous thoughts against Albion.
Los rag'd and stamp'd the earth in his might & terrible wrath!
He stood and stamp'd the earth! then he threw down his hammer in rage &
In fury: then he sat down and wept, terrified! Then arose
And chaunted his song, labouring with the tongs and hammer;
But still the Spectre divided, and still his pain increas'd!
In pain the Spectre divided: in pain of hunger and thirst:
To devour Los's Human Perfection, but when he saw that Los

39. Los's Spectre

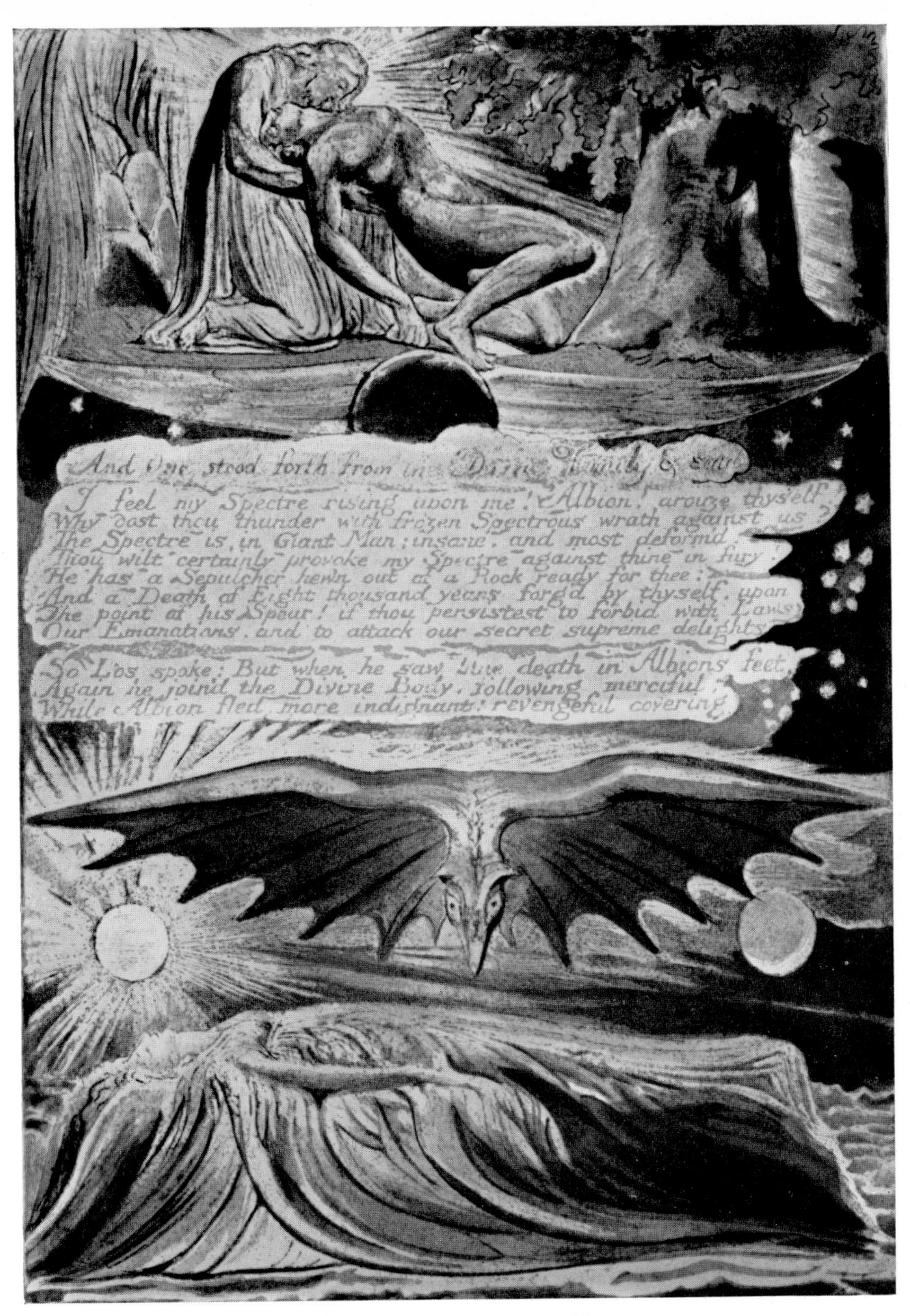

And One stood forth from the Divine
I feel my Spectre rising upon me! Albion! arouze thyself
Why dost thou thunder with frozen Spectrous wrath against us?
The Spectre is, in Giant Man; insane, and most deform'd.
Thou wilt certainly provoke my Spectre against thine in fury!
He has a Sepulcher hewn out of a Rock ready for thee:
And a Death of Eight thousand years forg'd by thyself, upon
The point of his Spear! if thou persistest to forbid with Laws
Our Emanations, and to attack our secret supreme delights
So Los spoke: But when he saw blue death in Albions feet,
Again he join'd the Divine Body, following merciful;
While Albion fled more indignant! revengeful covering

40. Los attempts to rescue Albion

41. Job's Nightmare

42. David delivered out of many Waters

43. Jesus refusing the Banquet

44. Newton and Orc

45. Newton

46. The House of Death

47. Blake's vision of Los

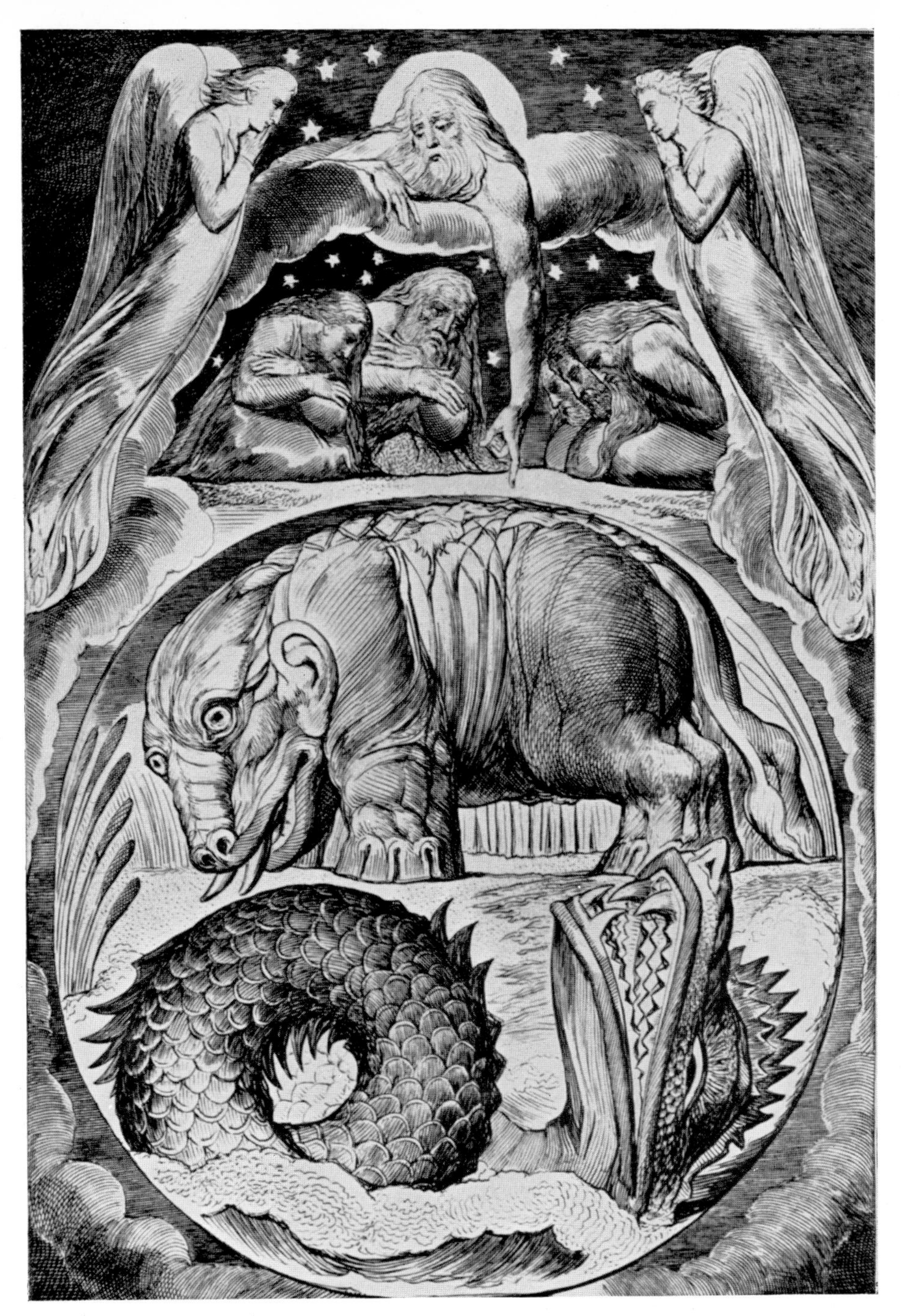

48. Behemoth and Leviathan

49. Milton prepares to descend

50. The star in Blake's left foot

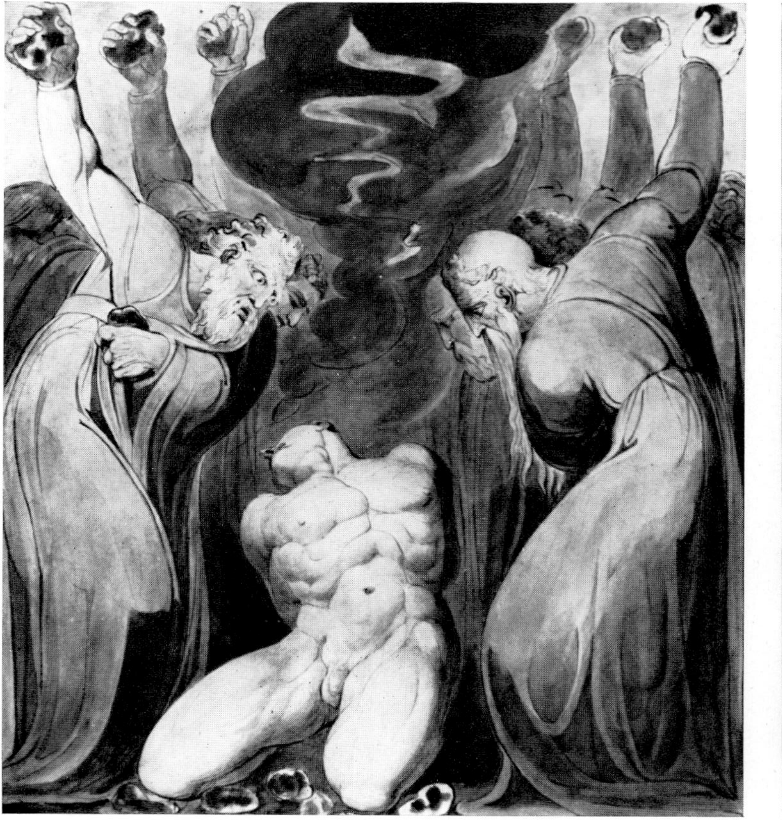

51. The stoning of Achan

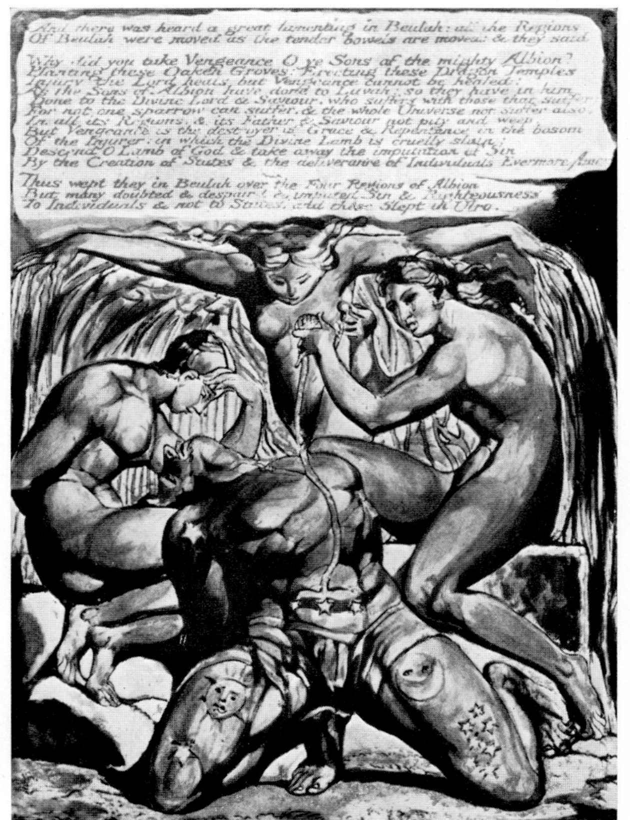

52. 'Thus wept they in Beulah'

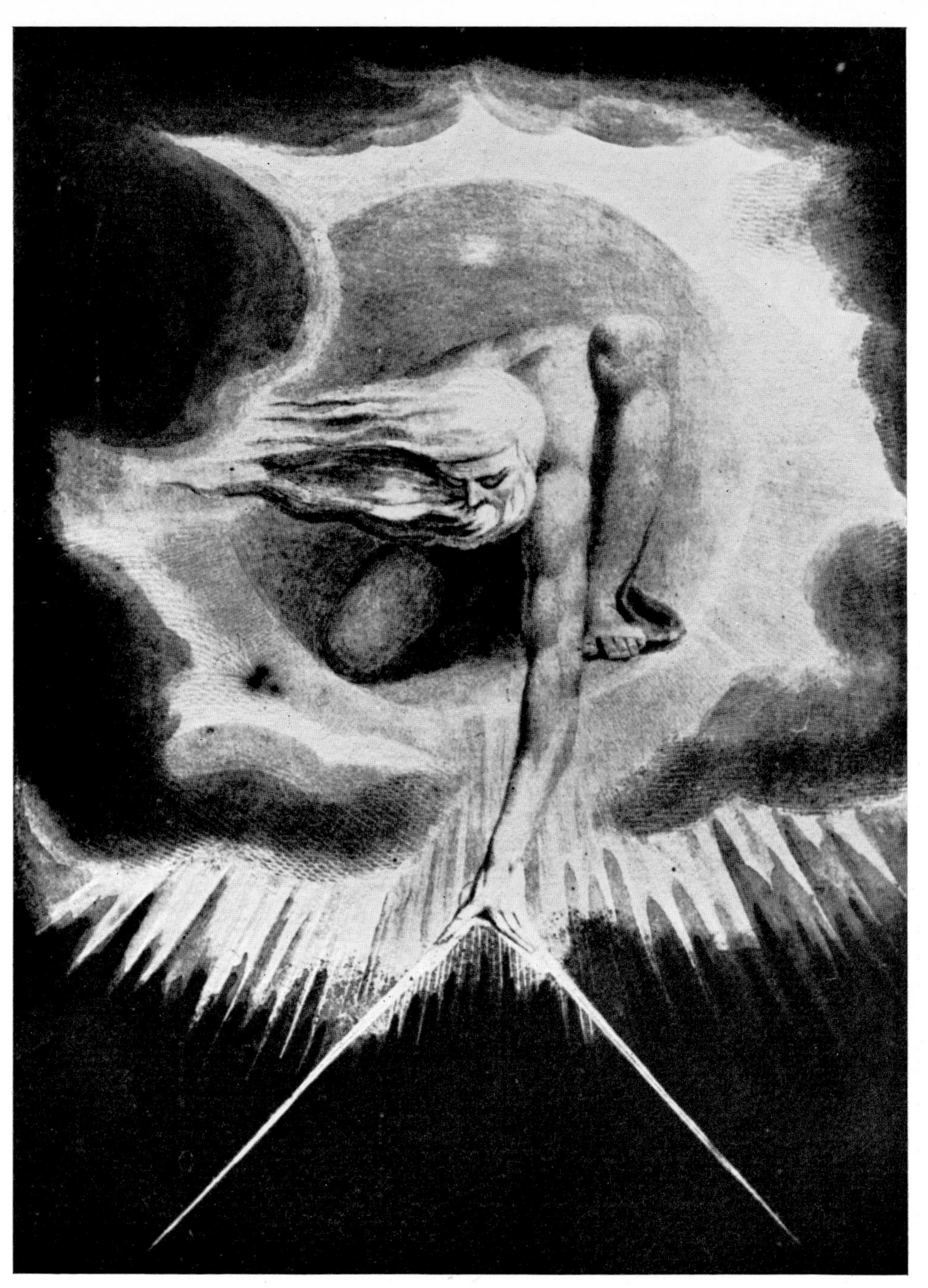

53. Urizen—Creator

54. The Arlington Court *Regeneration*

55. Regeneration (detail): The Writhing Group

56. Regeneration (detail): The two Chariots

57. Regeneration (detail): Jerusalem

58. Regeneration (central detail)

59. Regeneration (detail: right-hand portion)

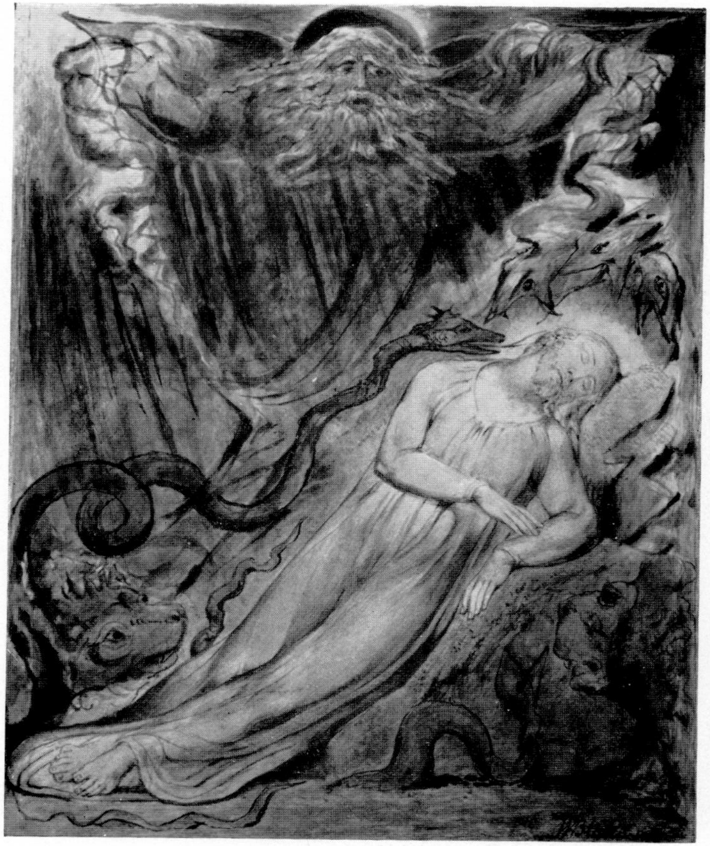

60. Jesus's troubled dream

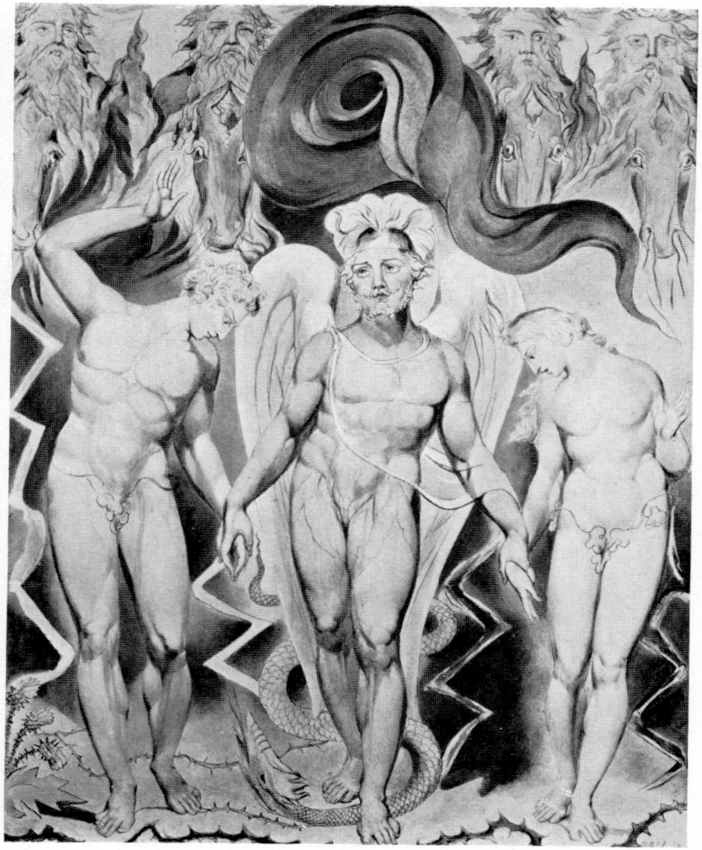

61. The Expulsion from Eden

62. Elijah about to ascend

63. 'When the Morning Stars sang together'

64. The Eagle of Inspiration

65. Vala and Jerusalem toe to toe

66. Jerusalem, Vala, and children

67. Bromion, Oothoon, and Theotormon

68. Oothoon and Theotormon

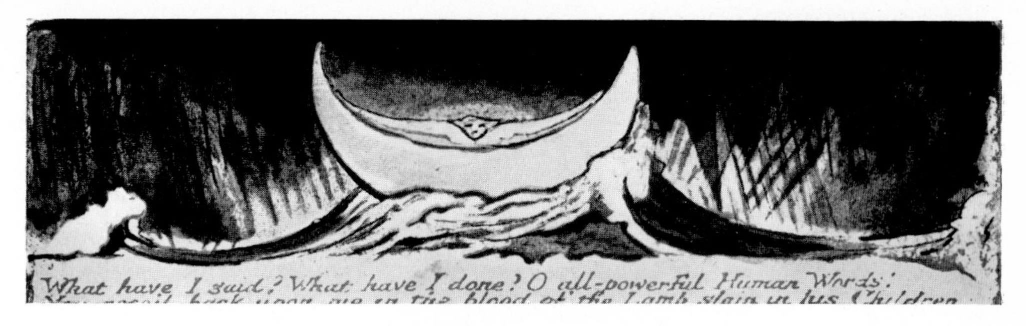

What have I said? What have I done? O all-powerful Human Words!

69. The Veil cast into the Atlantic

Jerusalem.
Chap: 2.
Every ornament of perfection, and every labour of love,
In all the Garden of Eden, & in all the golden mountains
Was become an envied horror, and a remembrance of jealousy:
And every Act a Crime, and Albion the punisher & judge.

70. The Lotus Flower

71. Hand in Flames

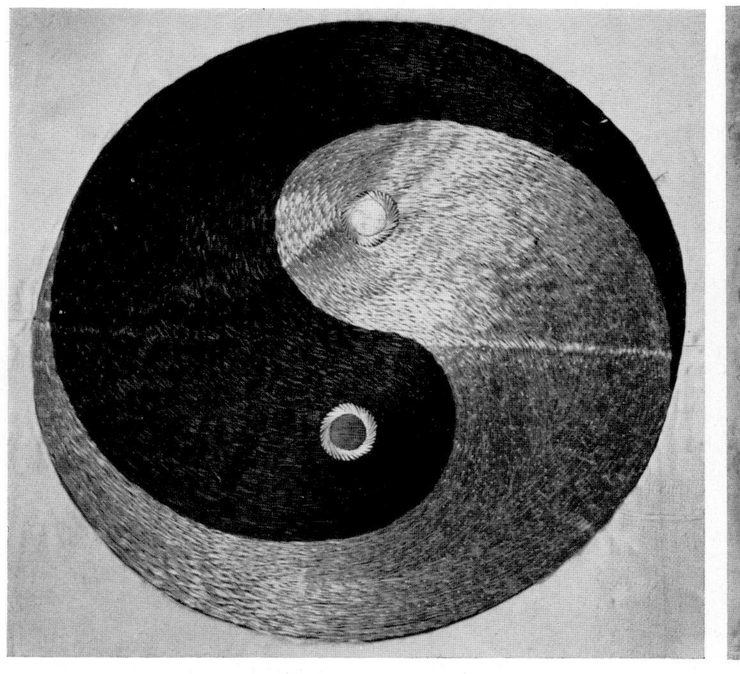

72. The T'ai-chi symbol

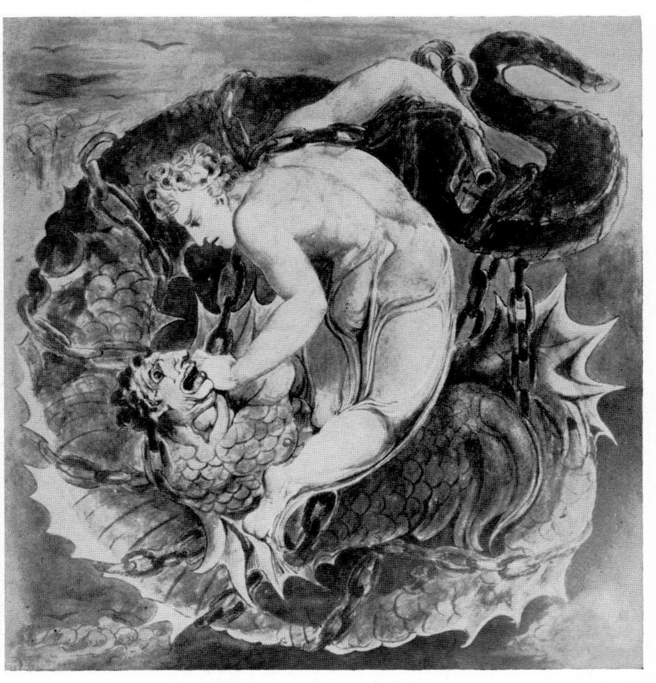

73. Michael and the Dragon

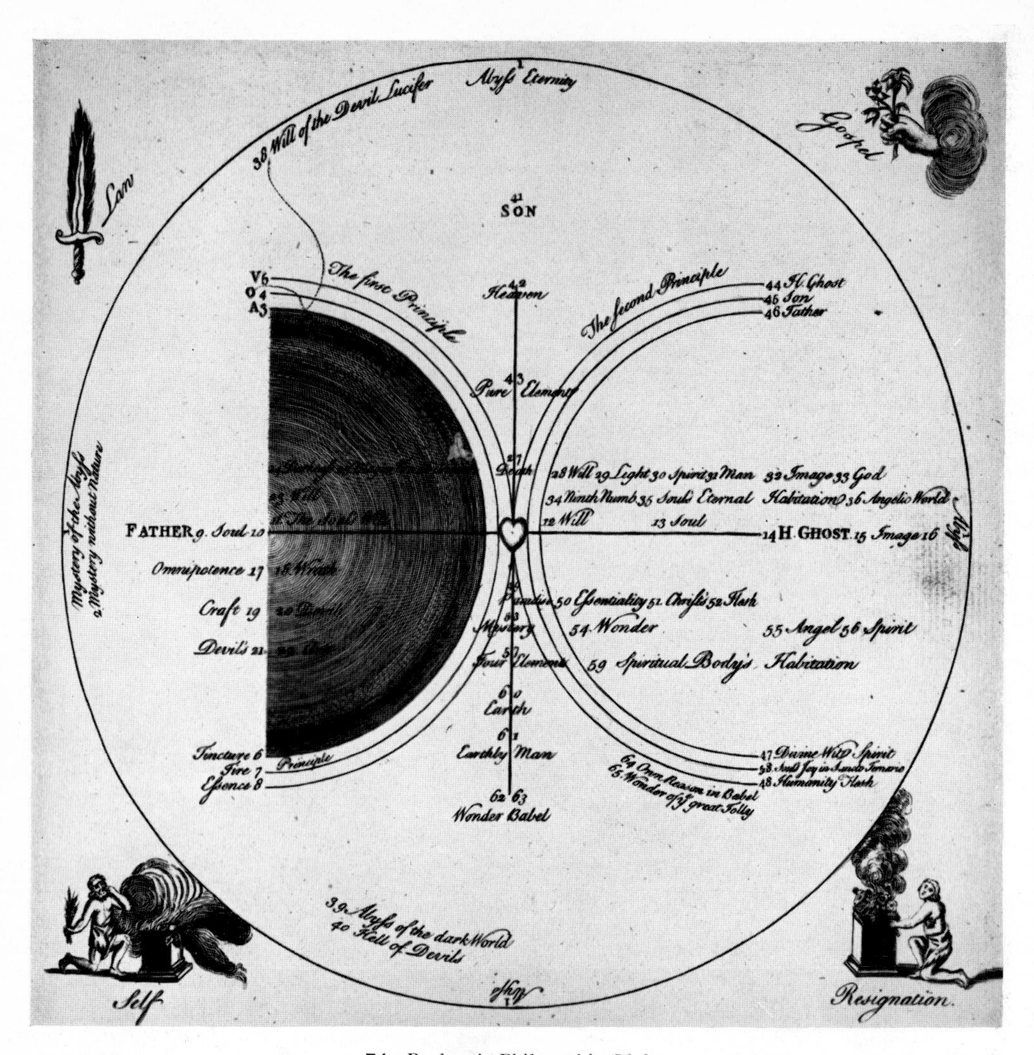

74. Boehme's Philosophic Globe

The Gods of the earth and sea,
Sought thro Nature to find this Tree
But their search was all in vain.
There grows one in the Human Brain

75. 'The Human Abstract'

Darkend the Atlantic mountains & their trumpets shook the valleys
Armd with diseases of the earth to cast upon the Abyss
Their numbers forty millions, mustring in the eastern sky.

76. Oothoon submerged

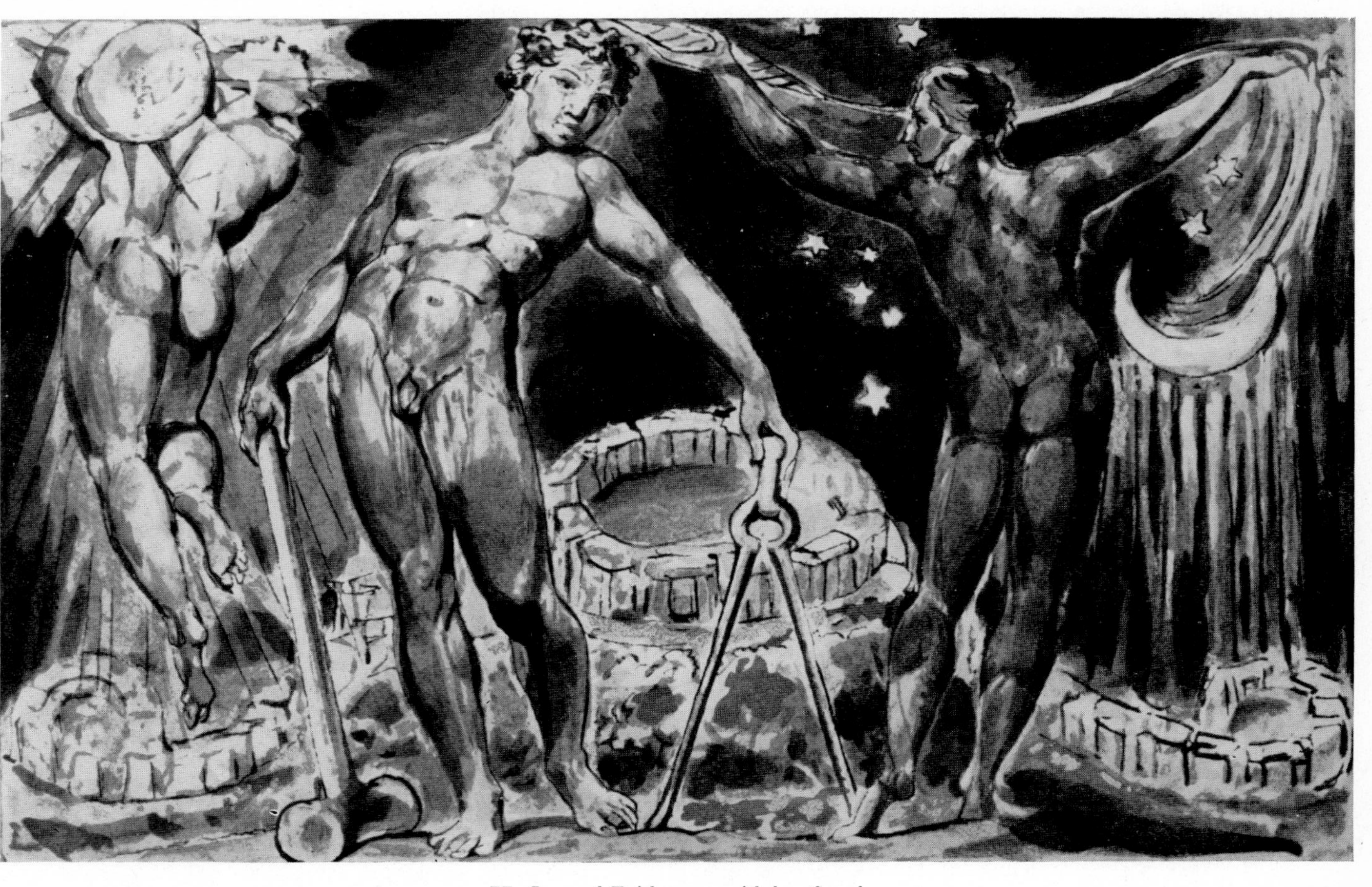

77. Los and Enitharmon with her thread